GENRE ANALYSIS:

THE GANGSTER, THE EVOLVED DETECTIVE AND *THE DARK KNIGHT*

BY

KAMUELA KANESHIRO, MA

WWW.KAMUELAKANESHIRO.COM

Genre Analysis: The Gangster, The Evolved Detective, and The Dark Knight
Copyright © 2014 by Kamuela Kaneshiro All rights reserved.

www.kamuelakaneshiro.com

No part of this book may be reproduced, scanned, or distributed in any printed or electronic form without permission. Please do not participate in or encourage piracy of copyrighted materials in violation of the author's rights. Thank you for respecting the hard work of this author.

Cover Design and Formatting by: Streetlight Graphics, LLC

This revised thesis was originally presented to the faculty of the Department of Communication at Hawaii Pacific University in partial fulfillment of the requirements for the Master of Arts in Communication

May 2014

©2018 Kamuela Kaneshiro

TABLE OF CONTENTS

Abstract 9
Overview of the Problem 11
    Statement of the Problem 12
    Purpose of Study 13
    Research Question 13
    Importance of Study 13
    Scope 14
    Definition of Terms 15
    Limitations 16
    Conclusion 16
Literature Review 17
    Mythology 17
    Mythology in the Modern Era 19
    The Western Genre 20
    The Vigilante Myth 22
    Spread of Vigilantism 23
    The Gangster Genre 24
    The Detective Genre 26
    The Evolved Detective Genre 28

    Film Noir 29

    Batman's Origins 33

    Gothic Fear 34

    Batman Beyond the Page 35

    The Films of Batman 36

    Reflections of Modern Times 40

    The P.A.T.R.I.O.T. Act 47

    The Joker as a Terrorist 58

    The Prisoner's Dilemma 62

    Methodology 65

    Semiotics 65

    Genres 67

    Conclusion 68

Methodology 70

    Purpose and Justification 70

    Study Design 71

    Assumptions 73

    Limitations 74

    Conclusion 74

Analysis of the Data 75

    The Opening Sequence and Film Noir 75

    The Attacks of September 11, 2001 77

    The Joker's Bank Robbery 77

    Terrorist Blending 78

    Game-Like Elements 79

    Terrorist: The Modern Other 79

    The Bat Signal 80

    The Color-Code System ... 80
    Batman as a Terrorist ... 81
    The Batman Copycats ... 82
    The Joker's Videotape ... 83
    Batman's Sonar Technology ... 84
    Terrorism Vs. Counterterrorism ... 85
    Batman Interrogates the Joker ... 86
    The Ticking Bomb Scenario ... 86
    Misinformation ... 87
    The Joker's "Prisoner's Dilemma" ... 87
    Film Noir and Fear ... 89
    The Gangster Genre ... 89
    The Evolved Detective Genre ... 90
    The Last Laugh ... 91
    Conclusion ... 91

Conclusion ... 92
    Recommendations ... 95
    Future Studies ... 95

References ... 97

ABSTRACT

Genre Analysis: The Gangster, The Evolved Detective and *The Dark Knight*

Kamuela Kaneshiro, B.A., M.A.

M.A. Communication, Hawaii Pacific University, Department of Communication

May 2014

Thesis Advisor. Dr. John Barnum

How the Christopher Nolan film *The Dark Knight* might reflect post-9/11 American culture. The film was compared to the film genres known as the Gangster genre and the Evolved Detective genre. Together these genres were analyzed along with the film style known as film noir in order to understand if *The Dark Knight* is a representation of post-9/11 culture. In the end it was discovered that Batman like many superheroes, is a highly adaptable character that reflects American values. It was concluded that *The Dark Knight* did reflect a post-9/11 world. *The Dark Knight* is a good example of American ideals and can serve as a working modern myth.

Keywords: vigilante justice, the prisoner's dilemma, the ticking bomb scenario, post 9/11 culture, the gangster genre, the evolved detective, gothic fear, film noir

Genre Analysis: The Gangster, The Evolved Detective and *The Dark Knight*

CHAPTER 1
OVERVIEW OF THE PROBLEM

A BLEAK MOMENT IN RECENT AMERICAN history is the attacks of 9/11. This incident devastated America and affected the world. It also affected American policy and culture. Americans struggled for a return to order. Zehnder & Calvert (2003) wrote, "The trauma of such loss of life and of unexpected destruction left many Americans feeling victimized, looking for answers and dealing with unimaginable bereavement. People looked for heroes to help them overcome what seemed to be insurmountable obstacles" (p. 3).

For many people 9/11 was a tragic surprise that devastated millions and generated memories of another era's bleak surprise, the bombing of Pearl Harbor. During these times people might have been worried or lived in fear. They needed something to help them rally to the call of war. Morrison (2011), stated that he grew up during the late 60's an era known as the atomic age, a time when the largest threat to the world was "the bomb." As a child Morrison needed something to believe in because all the news and talk was just about "the bomb." The bomb scared Morrison and caused him to worry about his friends, family and future. America during the 1930s was a nation going through the turmoil of the great depression, while boat loads of immigrants arrived only to face rough living conditions and very few jobs. Americans were searching for a way to distract themselves from their troubles of poverty and an uncertain future. The answer for a nation embarking on war was a larger-than-life concept to build a nation's morale, provide hope to international citizens like Morrison, and settle the nerves of an anxiety ravished America. This aid would arrive in the form of comic book superheroes. Schlesinger (2010) stated that the Golden Age of comics was born with Action Comics #1 starring a comic book superhero known as "Superman".

The success of Superman resulted in more superheroes being created. In 1939 a darker hero that was a combination of other heroes like The Shadow who utilized "gothic fear" as a weapon was created. This hero was known as "Batman." Over time the Batman character and mythos would undergo many retellings, expanding its reach beyond comic book culture to mainstream audiences, through the mediums of television and film. As of this writing, the Batman film franchise includes two serials and eight feature films. One of the films in this franchise was Christopher Nolan's 2008 *The Dark Knight*. *The Dark Knight* was a great success, praised by critics, the public and according to Box Office Mojo (2008) the film's budget was $185 million dollars but generated over $1 billion dollars. *The Dark Knight* is a sequel to the 2005 film *Batman Begins*. Fisher (2006) wrote that these films were the latest Batman incarnations based on the 1939 Detective Comics issue, which introduced the crime fighting hero known as the Batman.

Armed with his gadgets, physical training, deduction skills and following a highly structured code of ethics, Batman was a normal man with no super powers that the common man could relate to. Counterpoint to Batman's rigid control was the psychopathic, white-faced Joker. While Batman does have many enemies, the lanky Joker is considered to be one of "The Bat's" most unpredictable and deadliest. The two have a long track record of run-ins, as of this writing Nolan's *The Dark Knight* was the most recent. Nolan's dark, realistic grittiness of *The Dark Knight* not only pitted Batman against the Joker, but Ip (2012), wrote that *The Dark Knight* is a representation of a post-9/11 counterterrorism world, where people did not know who to trust, and faced the looming threat of terrorism on a daily basis.

STATEMENT OF THE PROBLEM

After the events of September 11, 2001, the world saw an influx of darker films such as *V for Vendetta*, *Taken* and *Munich*. The characters in these films seemed to be haunted by a type of angst; the cinematography was darker than the established "film noir" style, with filters adding a hue to scenes, and themes dealt with realist issues that reflected current events that might have been spoken about on the nightly news. If *The Dark Knight* is a post-9/11 film, what issues does it address and were these post-9/11 themes always present in the Batman mythos?

PURPOSE OF STUDY

This paper will examine *The Dark Knight* as a post-9/11 cultural artifact and the date of September 11, 2001 as a point in history which might have caused a cultural shift in America. This study shall attempt to find the extent of this cultural shift's effect on *The Dark Knight*.

RESEARCH QUESTION

How did a successful comic book film based on a 1939 superhero known as Batman, end up reflecting a post-9/11 American culture?

IMPORTANCE OF STUDY

Batman has been around since 1939, his success can be linked with a deeper connection to his story and possibly our cultural psychology. Batman was not the first comic book superhero; Batman was a successful follow up to Superman. While Batman started as a comic book character, over time he became "pop culture." According to Marsh (1999), there is a connection between pop culture and our psychology, "popular culture can be a site for exploring some of the most powerful elements of our psyches and the discourses of superheroes" (p. 119). Marsh's findings give us the first glimpse of a deeper connection between comic books, pop culture and our subconscious.

Smith (2009), wrote that in the 1940's Batman became a pop culture icon. During this time before commercial television, comic books were being turned into theatrical serials. Nineteen forty-three saw Batman translated onto the silver screen in the serial *Batman*. The success of this serial spawned the 1949 serial *Batman and Robin*. Batman would eventually make it to television with the 1966 *Batman* live action television series starring Adam West. This Batman utilized 1965's sweeping colorization of television shows to great effect. Over the top colored costumes and inserted comic bubbles of "Biff" and "Pow" during the fight sequences added a campy comic book edge. The program's overall design reflected the current mood of television where fantasy and enchantment reigned. At this time television shows like *Mister Ed, Bewitched* and *The Addams Family* presented a world where talking animals, witches and bizarre situations were common place.

In 1989 film director Tim Burton reinvented the image of Batman with his film *Batman*, which was a dark fantasy vision of Batman, Gotham City and the Joker. Burton's 1992 sequel *Batman Returns* produced a darker image of Batman with his enemies Catwoman and the Penguin. Tim Burton decided to leave the Batman franchise and Joel Schumacher directed Batman's following films: 1995's *Batman Forever*, 1997's *Batman & Robin* which seemed to mix elements of the campy 1966 live action television show with Burton's dark fantasy.

Film director Christopher Nolan created the 2005 *Batman Begins* which rebooted the Batman film mythos and introduced a gritty realism that seemed to have been lacking in Batman's previous incarnations. Nolan then made the sequel 2008's *The Dark Knight* and completed the storyline with 2012's *The Dark Knight Rises*. Nolan's films not only contained creative realistic interpretations of Batman and the characters of Batman's Universe. But throughout the films Nolan decided to focus on the real identity of Batman, Bruce Wayne. Through Wayne the audience was shown a victim who experienced interpretive acts of terrorism, based on real terrorism that the audience witnessed from living in a post-9/11 world. Schlesinger (2010) stated these parallels as "explicit" (p.138).

SCOPE

This paper will examine Nolan's *The Dark Knight* as an artifact with some time being spent on *Batman Begins*. This is mainly because *Batman Begins* is a "part 1" film or an "origin film". Most origin films need to spend most of their limited time on exposition so the audience may become familiar with the film's universe. This might include but is not limited to how things work, a brief history of how things got to this point in the film and who the characters are. This exposition is in addition to the film attempting to create an intriguing plot. This plot will be the centerpiece of the film. *The*

Dark Knight is a "part 2" film, the sequel to *Batman Begins* which took place about one year after *Batman Begins*.

Unlike origin films, sequels may not need to spend time going into the level of detail that origin films must, because the film's universe was already established in the origin film. While both *Batman Begins* and *The Dark Knight* have events which could be interpretations of a post-9/11 world, it might be seen that *Batman Begins* introduced post-9/11 concepts while *The Dark Knight* boiled down these ideas and put them into physical form. Due to this, more attention was placed upon the characters and plot in *The Dark Knight* than *Batman Begins*. With the additional time spent on plot and characters, this paper has more post-9/11 aspects to consider and examine. The methodology used in this paper will be generic application, a specific form of generic criticism in order to research if there are any established film genres that might be applied to *The Dark Knight*.

The identification of film genre might provide insight into connections between *The Dark Knight* and a post-9/11 culture. This paper will also be analyzing the events on and after September 11, 2001 in an attempt to identify similarities between real life events that happened, as well as representations of these activities in *The Dark Knight*. This paper will also examine:

- What is film genre and how can it be useful?
- What type of film genre should be applied to Batman and the Joker?
- What is film noir?
- Torture as a post-9/11 benchmark for security and intelligence gathering.
- The "Ticking Bomb Scenario" and "The Prisoner's Dilemma" in post-9/11 culture.

DEFINITION OF TERMS

The selection of terms was based on their connection with Batman's tactics and the Joker's actions in the films *Batman Begins* (2005) and *The Dark Knight* (2008).

Enhanced Interrogation Techniques: The use of torture on a suspect.

Gothic Fear: Using gothic elements like superstition, and symbols to scare others.

The Prisoner's Dilemma: A sociological experiment that attempted to show the advantages of cooperation and the disadvantages of selfishness in human nature.

The Ticking Bomb Scenario: A debate topic that argues the pros and cons of torturing a hostage. The scenario had a captured individual who planted time-bombs and refuses to disclose their locations. The debate arises as: should torture be administered to the captured individual in order to locate the bombs at the risk of the individual's freedoms and possible false information?

LIMITATIONS

Due to the vastness of the Batman mythos, attention will be focused on Christopher Nolan's post-9/11 films: *Batman Begins* and *The Dark Knight*. This paper will also be examining other post-9/11 aspects of: vigilantism, terrorism, the use of fear, film noir, torture and "The Prisoner's Dilemma."

CONCLUSION

This section provided an outline that will be used in order to establish a connection between *The Dark Knight* and its reflecting a post-9/11 culture. The following section will present material that has been written on these topics.

CHAPTER 2
LITERATURE REVIEW

THIS CHAPTER EXPLORES ACADEMIC LITERATURE on mythmaking, heroes, villains, genre analysis, film noir stylistics, and the evolution of Batman and the Batman franchise.

MYTHOLOGY

The philosopher Joseph Campbell explored various myths around the world in an attempt to discover the importance of myth to society. Due to the importance and density of Campbell's (1968) *The Hero with a Thousand Faces*, the following shall attempt to summarize key elements found in his writing. Campbell created a concept known as "monomyth." The monomyth has also been referred to as "The Hero's Journey." Campbell created some of the hero's journey on Freudian concepts, Jungian archetypes and van Gennep structuring. The definition of monomyth (the hero's journey) follows the story of the hero in a common world. The hero is presented with "a call to adventure," which spurs the hero to leave his common world for a different and strange world. In these new surroundings the hero faces tests and trials titled "a road of trials." Once the hero has completed his most severe challenge, the surviving hero is rewarded with a "boon."

The hero then returns to his original common world with the boon and uses the great gift to improve his common world. Campbell (1968) believed that myth was important for a society because the stories of myth helped members of society cope with changes and challenges they may encounter in the course of their lives. Parallels might be seen between Campbell's hero's journey and the mythos of Batman.

While the retellings of Batman's story change, the Batman mythos remains the same: Bruce Wayne's parents were killed during a mugging leaving Bruce Wayne as an orphan child. Bruce Wayne vowed vengeance upon crime and dedicated his life to improving himself in order to combat crime. Bruce Wayne traveled the world and returned to his crime ridden home of Gotham City, where he adopted the secret identity of Batman, an expert martial artist armed with high tech gadgets who attempts to stop crime and make Gotham City a better place. The call to adventure was the unfortunate murder of Bruce Wayne's parents, which spawned Bruce Wayne's vengeance. The road of trials were the various obstacles of training that Bruce Wayne performed to improve himself. The boon was the worldly knowledge of martial arts and criminology that Wayne returned to Gotham City with.

Schatz (1981) stated that myths help the reader/audience with issues that they may face. "Myth should not be identified by its repetition of some classical content or 'pantheistic' story. It should be perceived through its cultural function - a unique conceptual system that confronts and resolves immediate social and ideological conflicts" (p. 262). Myth is an important aspect for society because of the lessons that it teaches members of society. The story of the Batman mythos may be interpreted as a wronged man dedicated to outdoing himself in order to improve society for the better by taking a stand against crime. Unlike other heroes gifted with super-human powers such as: Superman, Wonder Woman and The Flash, Batman is an ordinary individual on a quest of self perfection.

Bilandzic, Sukalla, Herrmann and Kinnebrock (2008) explored the importance stories and myths have on culture. They pointed out that knowledge of norms, lessons and values told through stories and myths may make them easier for an audience to understand and remember, if presented in a narrative form "Knowledge presented in narrative format is more easily comprehended and remembered... It is not uncommon to assume that humans are hard-wired to think in stories and to organize their knowledge in stories" (Bilandzic et al., 2008, p. 3). The Batman mythos implied that life includes difficult hardships. But if an individual is determined, he or she could go on to do great things. The Batman mythos asks the reader to take a stand for good instead of bad.

MYTHOLOGY IN THE MODERN ERA

Stories and myths are a vital tool for not only understanding ourselves but the creator's culture as well. There are a number of characteristics that uniquely link Batman with American culture. Wanzo (2009) stated that the superhero was created with aspects that are considered ideal U.S. culture characteristics. "Revisions of the superhero mythos are often interrogations of what kinds of identities and ideologies are cast as ideal in U.S. culture and, as such, are useful springboards for discussing ideological mainstays informing narratives of good American citizenship" (p. 93). American culture is using the superhero to teach ideal cultural citizenship to its audience and presenting it in a narrative form to be easier to remember. Batman through all his interpretations fights crime in an attempt to improve the safety of Gotham City: readers might imply that they should side with good. If they do not, then the police or a force like Batman might stop them. Batman's hard work and determination allowed him to accomplish his dream. Some might consider this a connection with the promise of the "American Dream," where it did not matter who you were or what you did. With hard work and determination anyone could accomplish their dreams.

Superheroes also reflect the current aspects of their time. Schlesinger (2010) pointed out that comic book writer Alan Moore said that superheroes are modern myths. Moore stated that "Superheroes are contemporary manifestations of the mythological gods of yore, who reflected the tenor of their times as succinctly as contemporary pop-culture obsessions do ours" (as cited in Schlesinger, 2010, p. 40). Superheroes like Batman serve as an example of modern myths that also reflect our current culture.

Dittmer (2005) recounted what comic book creator Stan Lee said about how creators are influenced by the world around them. Lee stated:

> Everything that is happening at the time a story is written has an effect on that story, whether an obvious effect or a subliminal one. We [creative staff] are all influenced and affected by the events of the world around us at any given time. (As cited in Dittmer, 2005, p. 632)

The Batman comic book series began in 1939 with Batman stopping criminals and organized crime. The comic book company was Detective Comics who would later shorten their name to DC Comics. During this time America was still in "The Great Depression," recovering from the 20s gangster era and seeing immigrants leaving their war-torn home countries to make their pilgrimages to America with the hope of fulfilling the American Dream.

Further, Schatz (1981) explained that certain Hollywood films contain two repetitive aspects: problem-solving strategies and a heroic persona attempting to establish a type of order.

> Consider the basic similarities between those two activities: how the society at large participates in isolating and refining certain stories, the fact that those stories are essentially problem-solving strategies whose conflicts cannot be fully resolved (hence the infinite variations), the tendency for heroic types to mediate the opposing values inherent within the problem, and the attempt to resolve the problem in a fashion that reinforces the problem, and the attempt to resolve the problem in a fashion that reinforces the existing social and conceptual order. Genre films, much like the folk tales of primitive cultures, serve to defuse threats to the social order and thereby to provide some logical coherence to that order. (p. 263)

Schatz (1981) implied a connection between genre films and "folk tales" or myths. Genre films contain a problem which a hero must rise to solve. Campbell's (1968) hero's journey referred to this as the call to adventure and hero. Schatz (1981) stated that genre films also had a lesson that was being presented to the audience. This lesson would help retain social order. Myths usually contained a lesson to be remembered to help the individual with social order as well as beliefs of their culture.

THE WESTERN GENRE

Schatz (1981) wrote that the "Western Hero" is a hero who attempts to civilize a savage land.

> The Western hero, regardless of his social or legal standing is necessarily an agent of civilization in the savage frontier. He represents both the social order and the threatening savagery that typify the Western milieu. Thus he animates the inherent dynamic qualities of the community, providing a dramatic vehicle through which the audience can confront generic conflicts. (p.26)

Schatz (1981) explained that the Western hero embodies both order and savagery. Campbell's (1968) returned hero with the boon embodied both the order of his culture and the savagery from the outside world he experienced. With this, the returned hero attempts to forge a new and better world within his culture. Batman returned from his worldly training and is attempting to forge a better Gotham City, yet his actions are a combination of the legal order of justice and the savage criminal activity he pursues. The western genre provides solutions to conflicts that may be similar to some issues that a modern American community might face.

To summarize Jung's (2010) work from page 27, Westerns provided a venue to display the values of individualism and society. Westerns also created a formula for a film that encourages violence. The Western genre provided the audience with symbolic expressions of conflicting social issues. These social issues increase in tension till there is a violent action, which resolves the problem. The audience lives vicariously though the deeds of the hero. To the audience's delight, the hero encounters social issues presented in a symbolic way, which the hero physically deals with. In the film, *The Dark Knight*, social questions were written into the film, these were: "The Ticking Bomb Scenario" and "The Prisoners Dilemma". Social issues created in a post-9/11 climate were also included which were: the right to covertly spy on innocent citizens and the use of fear upon a populace.

Ip (2012) connected the Batman mythos with "popular culture" and American Westerns.

> Batman's story fits the classic narrative of the virtuous vigilante violently cleansing a cowering community beset by an impotent legal system. This type of story has a long

pedigree in American popular culture, and it includes the tales of heroic gunslingers of the old West. (p. 226)

Ip (2012) implied that Batman's story is rooted in American pop culture. Included in this assumption is that the vigilante entered a weak community and restored order. The character of Batman is always attempting to restore order to Gotham City.

Schatz (1981) stated that a vengeful hero is different from the Western hero, but they do have similarities.

> [The vengeful hero] does share with the classic hero his characteristic function: he is an isolated, psychologically static man of personal integrity who acts because society is too weak to do so. And it is these actions that finally enforce social order but necessitate his departure from the community he has saved. (p. 57)

The Western hero is usually a loner with high integrity who tries to restore order from the savageness because the community is too weak, however the Western hero flees from the community possibly because order has been restored and because of his loner mentality. At various times during the film, *The Dark Knight*, Batman's vigilante actions were illegal and something that would be dealt with at a later time. James Gordon said that protocol was to arrest Batman. Harvey Dent said that Batman was going to answer for his actions to the people of Gotham City. At the end of *The Dark Knight*, in order to fully restore order, Batman took responsibility for the Joker's killings. Once the city's order was restored, Batman could be dealt with causing the citizens to rise up against Batman because he was a criminal and the city no longer needed him.

THE VIGILANTE MYTH

While Batman is not an ordinary hero, he is a hero from the "vigilante myth". According to Jung (2010), the vigilante myth occurs when the hero is personally wronged and when society offers him no answers, the hero takes matters into his own hands.

> The hero or his loved ones are personally assaulted and society proves unable to provide justice, which is the justification for his actions… Vigilantism refers to the method of taking the law into one's own hands. The vigilante decides on his own authority who deserves what punishment for what crime. (p. 30 - 31)

Bruce Wayne lost his parents and childhood. Wayne created the identity of Batman to combat crime as a type of vengeance for the injustice done to him; this personal loss is similar to the loss explained in the vigilante myth.

In contrast, Tuman (2010) said myths are partial truths and exaggerations that have a lasting impact on our culture.

> Myths are fabrications crafted from analysis and ideas of half or partial truths. As fabrications, they become exaggerations or morph into claims that have little basis in fact. When employed in popular culture, however, they can have a lasting impact on public beliefs and discourse. (p. 191)

However, the longevity of myths shows that certain aspects resonate through time and are similar to time capsules that provide a reflection of their cultures. This repetitiveness implies pertinence to Campbell's (1968) work with Jung's (2010) archetype paradigm.

SPREAD OF VIGILANTISM

Batman was connected to what Jung (2010) called the "vigilante myth." There is a danger to vigilantism because vigilantism has the potential to spread. Desai (2004) explained that a small group of vigilantes have the potential to expand into a larger group that questions the established social order. "A vigilante movement which is born pressing a very narrow grievance or demand can rapidly [radicalize] and grow into a movement that questions the legitimacy of the entire social and political order" (p. 26). In the film *The Dark Knight* Batman motivated the citizens of Gotham City to stand up against crime.

This caused a group of copycats dressed as Batman to attempt to physically stop crime. Unlike Batman, these "Batman Copycats" were not as skilled as Batman, they did not have Batman's equipment. The copycats also did not have Batman's ethical code of not killing criminals. As a result, these copycats were putting themselves in danger and they were also armed with guns, which could potentially kill the criminals they were attempting to stop. Batman stopped the copycats and the criminals the copycats were trying to stop. Batman started as one individual and against his will, others started following his example of stopping crime.

When explaining the film *V for Vendetta*, Jung (2010) pointed out that the "vigilante myth" provides a vigilante the leeway for using excessive force. Jung also commented that combining the vigilante myth with a western grounds the character in real issues. "The [vigilante] myth sets up the syntactic expectation related to the significance of violence as normative solution, as well as the cultural significance of the Western as a catalyst of contemporary conflicts of values and attitudes" (p. 31). Due to the excessive nature of the vigilante myth, it justifies the character of Batman's violence as a normative solution and a necessary tool.

The Dark Knight Batman's absolute rule was that he will not kill a person. Just because he will not kill someone this does not mean he will not physically abuse them, *The Dark Knight*'s Batman beat up criminals including Batman copycats. Batman also physically tortured The Joker and a mob boss. However, at the end of the film Batman threw the Joker off the building, but saved him in order to stay true to his code of not killing people.

THE GANGSTER GENRE

As there are Western and vengeful heroes, there are also villains. Schatz (1981) stated that the role of the gangster genre was that of a violent criminal whose conflicting mindset was his own undoing. The gangster utilizes guns, cars, phones and other things to aid in his rise to power. However, the gangster's ultimate failure is due to the struggle between individual success and common good. This internal imbalance may put the gangster in more danger to himself than others. The genre also has the city, which plays a larger role as the representation of the faceless mass of citizens that occupy it. The city also stands as a symbol of order. "But somehow the massive, unthinking city, that concrete embodiment of civilization and urban order, is more powerful than either the self-reliant criminal or the generally inept police who pursue [the gangster]" (p. 85). During Nolan's *The Dark Knight*, the Joker admits that his weapons are guns, knives, gasoline and explosives. The Joker was able to successfully rise in power ultimately taking over organized mobs and Gotham City. However, at the end of the film the citizens [representing the city] stand up against the Joker by not taking part in his social experiment involving the two ferries. This scene was a modified version of "The Prisoner's Dilemma" and was the Joker's most disappointing defeat in the film because he was proven wrong about the citizens of Gotham.

Farber (1999) wrote that the gangster is a dark version of the American mythos.

> The gangster film is only a dark parody of the national myth. The gangster can be understood as a mutant variation on the American rugged individualist, living a perverted version of the American Dream; he acts out the wishes and values of the successful businessman, but with the high-sounding moral rationalizations stripped away. (p. 46)

This bleak doppelganger can act freely against America's social norms due to his lack of morals. The Joker during the film *The Dark Knight* was seemingly unstoppable. The Joker was always trying to make deals with the mob and attempting to convince Batman that he was wrong about the citizens of Gotham City and his moral code. While Batman had a high moral code, the Joker seemed to have a very low moral code.

Schatz (1981) observed the power of the gangster comes from his violent nature and lack of intellectual equals.

> The gangster's propensity for asserting his individual will through violent actions and self-stylized profiteering renders him an ideal screen persona. The fact that his assertiveness flaunts social order even heightens his individuality. He is surrounded by dull-witted underlings and pursued by inept

police in a confused moral climate that allows him ample opportunity. (p. 86)

In Nolan's *The Dark Knight*, the Joker had men in the Gotham City Police Department. The District Attorney Harvey Dent and Police Captain James Gordon had a meeting and both knew the department had questionable police officers. This caused Dent to mistrust the department. But Gordon admitted that he must work with what he had. The years of Gotham's weakened police force seemed to allow crime to fester. This was first seen in Nolan's *Batman Begins*. This situation caused the city to turn to a masked vigilante known as Batman for help.

Farber (1999) pointed out that the lesson learned from the gangster is that everyone must be punished for success.

> The gangster is doomed because he is under the obligation to succeed, not because the means he employs are unlawful. In the deeper layer of the modern consciousness, *all* means are unlawful, every attempt to succeed is an act of aggression, leaving one alone and guilty and defenseless among enemies: one is *punished* for success. This is our intolerable dilemma: that failure is a kind of death and success is evil and dangerous. (p. 48)

Towards the end of Nolan's *The Dark Knight*, the Joker is restrained by Batman and assumed to be arrested by police. Some of Batman's actions were also illegal and at the end of the film, the price of success over the Joker is that Batman had to become the villain in the eyes of the citizens of Gotham City.

THE DETECTIVE GENRE

Film genre is an evolving art form. According to Schatz (1981) following the gangster genre, the Western hero would evolve into the detective hero.

> In the early 1940s, the evolving gangster/urban crime formula and the burgeoning *film noir* style coalesced with other cultural factors to generate the most significant product

> of American expressionist cinema: the hardboiled-detective film. Distinct both from the classic gangster film, which focused on the criminal and his underworld milieu, and from the urban crime film, which traced the peace-keeping efforts of law-and-order agencies, the hardboiled-detective film assumed the viewpoint of the isolated, self-reliant "private eye." Like the classic Westerner, the hardboiled detective is a cultural middle-man. His individual talents and street-wise savvy enable him to survive within a sordid, crime-infested city, but his moral sensibilities and deep-rooted idealism align him with the forces of social order and the promise of a utopian urban community. (p. 123)

The detective is the Western hero's stylistic counterpart, who struggles in the fight to obtain a utopian society for his community. The character of Batman would struggle to restore Gotham City to its previous glory. This idealized Gotham City was the image remembered by Bruce Wayne as a child. In Nolan's *Batman Begins*, Wayne's father spoke of Gotham as a city that was always good to the Wayne family and the city needed help to return to its splendor.

At this point in cinema history Farber (1999) said that films became increasingly violent.

> [In some postwar American detective] genre films violence is intuitively celebrated as being consistent with the highest American ideals; violence almost seems to be the most appropriate expression of American aspirations. The drive for success is by nature violent. America exalts the *rugged* individualist, the self-made man who wins a place in the sun on his own initiative, regardless of the means that he uses in his struggle to the top. We reward the ruthless businessman, the robber baron, the man with the gun. (p. 46)

Due to America's competitive nature, violence seemed like an appropriate expression. We root for the successful, ruthless and violent individual.

Nolan's *The Dark Knight* contained Batman and the Joker, two individuals. Both were violent and had many small victories throughout the film.

THE EVOLVED DETECTIVE GENRE

The detective evolved into a darker version of previous incarnations. Schatz (1981) observed that the change in American culture created a vulnerable hero.

> The weather certainly changed in the 1960s, and cynicism, alienation, and frustrated romanticism reappeared, along with a nostalgic longing for the supposed simplicity of pre-'60s America. The detective's world was a more complex place now than it had been: instead of a "just" world war, there was Vietnam; instead of women waiting at home for their guys, there was the Women's Movement; urban blight had intensified to spawn ghettos and race riots… These and other cultural realities indicated a substantial revaluation of American ideology, and the detective-hero necessarily reflected the change in values. As did his '40s prototype, the screen detective of the 1970s accepted social corruption as a given and tried to remain isolated from it, still the naïve idealist beneath the cynical surface. But the new detective of the '70s inhabited a milieu he was unable to understand or to control… No longer a hero-protector, the detective in more recent films is himself the ultimate victim. (p. 149)

The detective's on screen safety was now never assured. He walked a line of uncertainty with increased danger, unrequited love, and faced becoming the "ultimate victim" personifying the only man with a solid moral compass in a corrupted world. Nolan's *The Dark Knight* Batman struggled with a number of such issues. Batman desired a relationship with childhood friend Rachel Dawes that would never come to be. Batman seemed like one of very few who had a strict moral code in Gotham City. Also in the final scene, Batman became one of the films ultimate victims when he claimed responsibility for the deaths caused by the Joker, which to the citizens of

Gotham City, tarnished his strict moral code, causing them to turn on him in the form of public mobs and police chasing him down.

FILM NOIR

Film noir is a style that attempts to establish the film's mood for the viewing audience. Ewing (1999) wrote,

> [film noir] had a dark style of visual presentation that combined gothic chiaroscuro lighting effects with an ambiguous and dislocated sense of space borrowed from the technical achievements of German Expressionism... *Serie noire* literature included French translations of Gothic novels and what is America called 'hardboiled' mystery novels. The world projected in *film noir* corresponded most closely to these latter works". (p. 73)

Film noir is a dark style that uses exaggeration and dramatic lighting. It spread into the world of detective stories and literature. Nolan's *Batman Begins* and *The Dark Knight* placed an emphasis of darkness and shadow. The Nolan Batman dwelled in the shadows and only appeared at night. The Nolan films also focused on the aspects of crime and legally sentencing criminals, as opposed to the Tim Burton and Joel Schumacher films which had Batman generally going against his moral code and killing his criminals. Previous films and television shows depicted a Batman who was focused on capturing the criminal with little regard as to the sentencing of the criminals after they were caught. Nolan's films with the exception of Ra's al Ghul and Harvey Dent/Two-Face had Batman stick with his moral code of no killing. To the points of Ghul and Dent, Batman did not directly kill them but he also did not save them. Nolan's Batman did not just capture his criminals; he had to have enough evidence to legally sentence them, a storyline that is similar to police procedure dramas.

Film noir or "black film" expressed the harsher and negative side of stories. This grittiness was explained by Schatz (1981).

> *Film noir*, as the style was dubbed by French critics, so dominated late 40s and early 50s films-principally those shot

> in black and white and involving the issue of urban order-that it came to identify both the narrative-cinematic style of those films and also the historical period during which they were produced. Generally speaking, *film noir* ("black film") refers to two interrelated aspects: visually, these films were darker and compositionally more abstract than most Hollywood films; thematically, they were considerably more pessimistic and brutal in their presentation of contemporary American life than even the gangster films of the early 1930s had been. (p. 111-112)

Schatz pointed out that film noir was more expressionistic and graphic than gangster films, skewing the image of American life. Nolan's films showed a Gotham City that was crime ridden with shanty residential dwellings. This Gotham City was part of a capitalist society but Gotham residents seemed to barely scrape by with their living conditions.

Sobchack (1998) explained noir as a stylistic contradiction.

> Dark in tone (if not always chiaroscuro in lighting), twisted in vision (if not always in framing), urban in sensibility (if not always in location), impotently angry and disillusioned in spirit (if not always in execution), noir circumscribed a world of existential, epistemological, and axiological uncertainty-and inscribed a cinema that film critics and scholars saw as an allegorical dramatization of the economic and social crises. (p. 133)

The filmic style of film noir reflected a lot of the anxiety and uncertainty that Americans faced due to the somber tones caused by economic depression, world wars and family uncertainty. Nolan's Batman films told the story of the crumbling Gotham City slowly being consumed by crime. At the center of this story was the use of fear as a weapon. Fear was used by the police, criminals and Batman all for different gains. The release of Nolan's films was in a post-9/11 world, which woke and slept in a state of fear.

With America's involvement in World War II, a cynical and pessimistic view began settling into the theater going public. Palmer (1997) explained that "film noir" was a film style that incorporated deep shadows and dramatic lighting. Noir was a style that combined metaphor with aspects of estrangement, alienation in a social content.

> Drawing out the night as both a time and a place within which noir's narratives were ideally situated, as well as a metaphor usefully symbolic in noir's oppositional scripts of estrangement and alienation... situated at the interface of discrete aspects of style and social content. (p. 57)

Through noir, filmmakers were able to create stark worlds that addressed social issues. The serious tone of films in this genre would resemble a world more realistic than film genres that have came before. Most of Nolan's films took place at night because that is the time of day that Batman emerges to confront crime. In *Batman Begins* the night is when the mob would do their dealings. In this film we discovered that Batman utilized the night to further his theatrics and his martial arts training. *The Dark Knight* presented a less crime ridden Gotham City due to Batman's work with aiding the police. Instead of organizing at night, the criminals now do their dealings in the day. Except the Joker, who worked during the night in order to get Batman's attention.

While film noir might confront political and social issues, noir is not "realist". Nelson (2008) insisted that noir is more existentialist than realist. This is important because noir should not be mistaken for realist style.

> Nobody thinks that noir is only realist in style; its look and sound are widely agreed to be expressivity too, and noir myth often is existentialist even more than it is realist. These complications can be advantages, however, because they can keep us from temptations simply to equate noir style with realist style. Popular forms of our political culture taken by convention to be more exclusively realist in style surely would include news and documentary. (p. 4-5)

Noir is not realist. Realist may be considered as another type of style. Noir is a style with elements of existentialist art presented in a slick narrative form. The Batman universe is fiction and it should not be considered realist.

Noir's format influences everything including the attitude of characters. Palmer (1997) stated that "noir anti-heroes" will likely favor darker physical deeds than honest actions. "When given the choice, noir anti-heroes inevitably choose betrayals and thefts, even murder, over honest toil and hard labor" (p. 60). Furthering the dark existentialist setting of noir, the hero is a reflection of his world, where he is illustrated more as a criminal than a hero. As mentioned earlier, Batman and his use of gothic fear made him seem more criminal than hero. In the Batman mythos, almost all of Batman's actions are considered illegal. Batman beats people up, damages property and violates many individual rights.

Vernet (1999) wrote about the importance of the opening sequence in film noirs. These moments are usually typified with tranquility because these are the tamest scenes in the film. In these first moments we can see the characteristics of the characters including the villain and hero. "The opening scenes of many film noirs designate and clarify the roles and attributions of each character… the strength and appearance of the heroes inspires no doubts in their abilities" (p. 59). In setting up the location, film noir also sets up the characters. *The Dark Knight* began with quiet opening credits before the first scene of the film. Steadily the noise and music began building with the introduction to Gotham City, The Joker, James Gordon and Batman all in the first few minutes. In these opening moments the audience was able to grasp the roles of each character. Each character also portrayed their abilities and were shown as competent.

Russell (1998) stated that horror film monsters were reflections of society.

> [The horror film genre] mediates between culture and ideology through an indirect mode of representation that formulates the tensions between the demands on the individual imposed by social order (as manifested through external social oppression) and by personal desire (internally held in check by emotional repression.)… horror films can function to reenact and reaffirm social repression and contain disorder and violence by eliminating the monster, which symbolically stands in for social disorder and rampant desire… Yet otherness itself expressed through the horror film

and its monsters may also serve to point to the breakdown and failure of repression as symptomatically expressed through a realization of unconscious desire for which the monster acts as a medium. (p. 237)

The horror film monster may be a symbol of a disorder disrupting the natural flow of society. *The Dark Knight*'s Joker attempted to show Gotham City that plans and rules are just illusions. The Joker tried to explain that plans were an extension of false control that society had on people. Comparatively, if something did not go to plan then people lost control. The Joker believed in living with no rules and anarchy was the only true civil order.

Nelson (2008) stated that while film noir was first developing, Batman comic books were already displaying signs of noir storytelling.

> The Superhero Saga invents superhuman powers to symbolize how the surprising resources of emerging movements can help a protagonist resist, escape, or even overthrow a totalitarian system of social control. This kind of tale appears with the Batman in American comics at the same time that noir films are taking shape, but it does not truly claim the big screen until Tim Burton brings the *Batman* (1989) onto the silver screen as neo noir. (p. 27)

Nelson (2008) believed that the superhero story was about individuals acting against social control. Early Batman comic book stories had the vigilante Batman fighting to save Gotham City from questionable social order.

BATMAN'S ORIGINS

While there have been changes to Batman's story of origin; the major details remained the same. As a child, Bruce Wayne witnessed the murder of his wealthy parents. Bruce vowed a life of vengeance against crime and dedicated his life to stopping crime. Bruce inherited his family's fortune and left Gotham City to see the world in order to prepare his body and mind for his crusade against crime. Bruce returned to his beloved Gotham

City and developed the secret identity Batman, a masked vigilante who works with police to take down crime in Gotham City.

Zehnder and Calvert (2003) studied the effects that heroes have on adolescent youths. With a Jungian point of view, Zehnder and Calvert stated that the hero archetype is a central character that separates from the ordinary world to experience various trials. The hero then returns changed and attempts to stabilize the ordinary world.

> The mythic hero's journey is compelling because it dramatizes the struggles that all people must face: that of choosing the right path of justice over the dark path of revenge. The hero's story often teaches a social lesson about how we should act and what we should aspire to when faced with adversity in our own lives. (Zehnder and Calvert, 2003, p. 6)

Batman's origin story of Bruce Wayne leaving Gotham and returning to restore order is similar to the hero archetype.

GOTHIC FEAR

Batman is known for his amazing intellect as well as his wide range of technological gadgets. But one of the primary tools in his arsenal was the use of fear on his enemies. Batman was not the first superhero to use fear. Fisher (2006) pointed out that Batman was always using "Gothic Fear" as a weapon for heroic justice since the original origin story. Gothic fear is the use of elements in Gothic literature such as various supernatural elements, symbols and theatrics in order to frighten others; Bruce Wayne eventually draws upon superstition, the image of a winged bat and aspects from the art of Ninjutsu to imply a supernatural fear of the unknown into his victims. Fisher quoted Bruce Wayne during the creation of his Batman identity, "Criminals are a superstitious cowardly lot, so my disguise must be able to strike terror into their hearts" (Fisher, 2006, para. 10). The Batman character is a hero that uses fear on his victims. The use of fear is double edged since his appearance could scare innocents as well. These aspects seem more suited for a villain than a hero.

Batman Begins had Bruce Wayne being taught by a group known as "The

League of Shadow." They taught Wayne to embrace his fear and ultimately use fear as a weapon against others. Wayne discovered that the league always chose justice no matter the cost. This went against Wayne's moral code of no killing and pitted Wayne against his brethren. Wayne returned to Gotham City and confessed a fear of bats. Wayne created Batman as a symbol of fear to criminals. In *The Dark Knight*, Batman is a successful symbol of fear that James Gordon uses to keep the city in order.

Batman may be a hero; however, he must perform a delicate balancing act to prevent himself from becoming a villain. Zehnder and Calvert (2003) stated that on the night of his parents' murder, Bruce Wayne formed a desire to become a hero as well as the psychological imbalance that could lead to Bruce Wayne becoming a villain.

> His struggle and triumph to heroism is born in the traumatic murder of his parents. Because of these events, Batman has the potential to be evil, to become dark and sinister if he succumbs to revenge even as he fights for justice. (p. 6)

The use of "Gothic Fear"; superstition imagery and implied supernatural ability on his enemies as well as the murder of his parents, describe Batman as a villain with psychological disorders.

BATMAN BEYOND THE PAGE

While Batman enjoyed success as a comic book, there was a world outside the pages of this limiting medium. Popular culture was a source of material in a world that consumes entertainment and it would provide Batman the ability to reach a larger audience. Zehnder and Calvert (2003) said that pop culture and superheroes were developed across the vastness of other mediums of multimedia, "In popular culture, this cultural script is developed and played repeatedly in films and television as superheroes triumph against all odds, including their victories over their own internal demons" (p. 3). Mainstream pop culture was the key in giving superheroes the exposure over vast mediums. During the early 1900s, superheroes made the leap from comic books to theater screens.

THE FILMS OF BATMAN

Pop culture's various mediums granted Batman his first exposure on the silver screen, jumping mediums from comic books to serial films. The Batman character had his big screen debut in the 1943 black and white serial *Batman* (1943). Smith (2009) observed that superheroes were being made into serial films and many of these films were successful.

> In addition to their immense visibility in the film business from the 1930s and 1940s and their role as early, typically financially successful, attempts at adapting comic books and comic strips to film, the style and format of these films have, by exploiting the serialized structure of the narrative modes of comic book visual rhetoric, arguably influenced the nature of the modern action film. (p. 13-14)

The serial *Batman* (1943) was released in theaters while America was fighting in World War II and had Batman as an employee of the US Government fighting a Japanese scientist known as Dr. Daka. Dr. Daka was a new Batman villain who never appeared in the Batman Universe before this time. The success of the serial generated the 1949 sequel *Batman and Robin*. The serial *Batman and Robin* (1949) was released years after the end of World War II (1945) and had Batman and Robin facing an unknown villain.

The Adam West Batman. With popular fantasy and science fiction shows on television, the Adam West 1966 *Batman* did its best to embrace a live action comic book look and feel. The opening sequence took a comic book appearance. While the show included the comic book action jargon: "Biff," "Pow," and "Bam" captions during the fight scenes. It also utilized the innovation of color televisions with bright, bold color costumes and sets.

The Adam West Batman faced his "gallery of rogues" during the television show, but his main villain was usually The Penguin. The Adam West Batman also jumped from television to film. Between television season 1 and 2, the Adam West Batman was featured in the 1966 *Batman: The Movie*. The Adam West Batman would be the first Batman in color on television and in film. The main villain Batman faced in *Batman: The Movie* was The

Penguin. The 60s culture had beatniks who introduced Eastern philosophy to Western minds and Andy Warhol's pop art. The Adam West Batman could be seen as a hip peacekeeper, educated with Eastern knowledge living in a world of over the top color. The next incarnation was Tim Burton's 1989 darker film *Batman*.

The Tim Burton Batman. American culture at the end of the 80s had family sitcoms (situational comedies) populating most of the television landscape. Sprinkled through television were science fiction shows about time traveling scientists and aliens who wanted to live peacefully among us. The Burton *Batman* (1989) consisted of the films *Batman* (1989) and *Batman Returns* (1992). A connection with family might be seen as a centerpiece in both films. Tim Burton's *Batman* reinterpreted the slaying of Wayne's parents and how Bruce fought to keep the families of Gotham safe from crime ravaged streets. *Batman Returns* took place during Christmas and had the Penguin longing to find his family, then threatening to steal all the first born children of Gotham City. Smith (2009) explained that Tim Burton's *Batman* successfully merged Batman into the realm of noir. The success was short lived as Batman slowly became more comedic.

> 1989 was a banner year for comic book films and was the next step in the progression of comic books as a profitable genre of cinematic adaptation. Tim Burton's Batman was the biggest hit of the year. However, by the third film in the series, Batman had returned to the parodic tone of the television series. (p. 17)

Burton's *Batman* had a decrepit Gotham City with a corrupt and inept police force. Burton's Joker aggressively rose to power through Gotham's mobs and the only person who could stop him was Batman. However, Burton's Batman did not concern himself with legal procedure. Batman was the cause of the Joker's death. While Burton's *Batman* contained elements of film noir, Burton's *Batman* skewed elements of the Batman mythos. 1995's *Batman Forever* was directed by Joel Schumacher, and was followed up in 1997 with *Batman & Robin*.

The Joel Schumacher Batman. As the turn of the century loomed, television during the late 90s was populated by comedies, and programs dealing with the unknown. However, primetime animated shows were growing in number. Schumacher's *Batman Forever* (1995) and *Batman & Robin* (1997) might have been seen as an attempt to make a modern version of the Adam West Batman universe and mixing it with Tim Burton's darkness. The result could be implied that Schumacher's Batman films were too cartoonish and at times self parodying. As of this writing IMDB.com had *Batman & Robin* rated "3.6 out of 10" with a "Metascore of 28 out of 100" (Internet Movie Database, 1997) Box Office Mojo (1997) had *Batman & Robin* as the worst rated grossing live action Batman film of the last thirty years. The Batman franchise would not see its next installment until Christopher Nolan's 2005 *Batman Begins*.

The Christopher Nolan Batman. During 2005, television programming might be seen as becoming serious with the success of long running "reality shows" like *Survivor*, *Big Brother*, and *American Idol*. The portrayal of reality became more interesting to audiences and the situation comedies lost their appeal. The steady stream of reality television shows from the late 90s dominated programming. The remaining television shows such as *Law and Order*, *CSI: Crime Scene Investigation*, and *Cold Case* dwelled in the realm of legal and/or police procedural dramas, while their characters struggle with a broken or dysfunctional family.

The tragic events of September 11, 2001 could have been a pivotal turning point of this change in popular culture. Nolan's Batman series of *Batman Begins* (2005) and *The Dark Knight* (2008) drew heavily from film noir, but presented a realistic story that attempted to keep Batman's world as believable as possible. In Nolan's Batman, the legal system and processing of criminals would be central. *Batman Begins* opens with the slaying of Wayne's parents, and how injustice was brought to their killer because he was a witness to bring down the mob who controlled Gotham City. Wayne considered killing their murderer, but was robbed of the opportunity by a mob's gunman. Wayne leaves Gotham but returns to clean up the city as Batman. Becoming Batman is a challenge as Wayne realizes that he needs particular equipment to help in his mobility across the city. Batman slowly recruited people to legally help him in his crusade and above all refused to kill anyone. Also for the first time, the live action Batman relied heavily on the assistance of Police Officer James Gordon, adding more of a cop drama angle to the Batman story. Batman also befriended Lucius Fox, a friend of Batman's father who acts as a friend and gadget maker. While Lucius Fox was a character in the Batman comics, this marked the first time Lucius was seen in a live action production.

In *The Dark Knight*, Batman attempted to legally take down the mobs controlling Gotham City with the help of Police Capitan James Gordon and District Attorney Harvey Dent. Throughout the film there was a struggle to keep legal proceedings legitimate in order to properly prosecute the guilty parties. Compared to the early comic book Batman, the serial Batman, the Adam West Batman, Tim Burton's Batman and Schumacher's Batman; Nolan's Batman was not colorful, more of a loner, and stressed the fact of helping the police legally arrest the criminals Nolan's Batman pursued.

Previous Batman incarnations had Batman killing or apprehending criminals with little or no evidence and it was assumed they would be put into jail. The legal proceedings aspect was hardly acknowledged. In his film review, Ebert (2008) explained how Nolan revolutionized not only Batman but how the film industry has reevaluated the potential of comic book films.

> 'Batman' isn't a comic book anymore. Christopher Nolan's *The Dark Knight* is a haunted film that leaps beyond its origins and becomes an engrossing tragedy. It creates characters we come to care about. That's because of the performances, because of the direction, because of the writing, and because of the superlative technical quality of the entire production… redefine the possibilities of the 'comic-book movie'. (Ebert, 2008, para. 1)

It took the genius of Nolan's films, sticking with the style of film noir and the original character of Batman, to reinvent the Batman film franchise and change the way Hollywood viewed comic book films.

The success of *The Dark Knight* could be attributed to a number of various aspects. As stated above, the style of film noir provided an excellent choice from an aesthetic and storytelling perspective. However, there are some that believe the storyline of *The Dark Knight* is the secret to its success. Kolenic

(2009) said that it was not just a story of good versus evil. But the story was able to make the audience sympathetic to each dueling side. "Its layered story in which the classic paradigm of order versus chaos is played out on the surface, and the unconscious logic of both sides of that dichotomy merge with viewers on a more profound and troubling level" (p. 1024). *The Dark Knight* was filled with contradictions. On the surface the vigilante known as Batman was ruling the city. Batman's appearance was mysterious and he looked like a horned creature of the night that appeared once the sun set. Batman was a "good guy" but he only came out at night, and performed a lot of illegal activity including using fear to maintain order in Gotham City. *The Dark Knight's* Joker was dressed in a fashionable suit as a smiling clown. While the Joker was killing people and breaking the law, he was trying to show Gotham City that they were living in a contrived world of illusion based on Batman's fear. This mayhem helped *The Dark Knight* audience understand the characters' motives, creating an internal debate over which side they should align themselves with.

REFLECTIONS OF MODERN TIMES

As stated earlier; comics, stories and myths are reflections of a society's culture. Schlesinger (2010) mentioned that *The Dark Knight* was successful because the storyline dealt with modern issues in a post-9/11 world.

> Nolan's Batman is a tortured soul who quests to defeat evil and protect the innocent (archetype), but must to the edge of his morals as he is confronted by the Joker, a terrorist whose motives and methods defy understanding and predictability [Post-9/11 historicity]. Indeed, these 9/11 parallels were explicit in both the film itself and the marketing campaign surrounding the film's release… while the story of terror and surveillance could have been told without superhero characters… the inclusion of the Batman and the Joker— recognizable icons of good and evil… made *The Dark Knight* a tremendous hit (p. 138-139).

This implies that *The Dark Knight* is a modern myth dealing with post-9/11 issues.

Post-9/11 Cinema. According to Dixon (2003) the events of 9/11 changed the landscape and culture of America. This change was influential in the development of post-9/11 films. "Just as [the events of] Pearl Harbor shaped the cinema of the 1940s, so September 11 will serve as the template for the new 21st century conflict" (p. 59). Studios, directors and producers now had a lot more to consider than just who was going to star in the film, they had to pay closer attention to aesthetics. Post-1940 cinema produced the gritty detective genre that was pessimistic with an unknown ending that was not guaranteed to be happy. These elements mirrored the uncertainty and anxiety of the time. Post-9/11 cinema should follow the threats of fear and reliance on multi-media that the world faced.

Jung (2010) stated as 9/11 unfolded, people claimed that it looked "just like a movie". Reality was imitating art, how can films continue to create product if everything would serve as a reminder of the images of 9/11?

> Cinema is challenged artistically. How is the fiction going to react to having become "real"... How can a visual medium represent a painful subject which hit home as close as it gets, both cinematically and culturally? Just as the representation is framed as being complicit by *depicting* violence, the audience is being complicit by *watching* these images. In other words: If terrorism is theater, who goes to see the show? The spectacular mode and its entertaining qualities only amplify this problem. (p. 16)

Filmmakers found it difficult trying to remain sensitive to the concerns that people had about the actual events of 9/11. The tragedy of 9/11 was so strong that it reshaped cultures and the images from the events looked like films or television fabrications. The challenge was to continue making fictitious films and television images, that terrorism corrupted by making real.

Ip (2012) stated direct connections between *The Dark Knight* and a post-9/11 world by comparing specific aesthetics found in the film, "grainy homemade videos, cell phone-detonated human bombs, burnt-out remains of buildings swarming with rescue workers-give the film a distinctly post-9/11 aesthetic" (p. 213). These elements helped to strengthen the connection between *The Dark Knight* reflecting the events of September 11, 2001 and a post 9/11 world.

Societal Ideologies. Bloodsworth-Lugo and Lugo-Lugo (2011) stated the aspect of how a film reflects the United States society can determine a trait of post-9/11 cinema.

> Our concern in this essay is not with whether films produced and released after September 11, 2001 are pessimistic, singular in vision, or encourage a warrior spirit, but with the way they embody, reflect, and portray a set of assumptions about United States culture at the start of the twenty-first century, as well as what they teach us about the ideological leanings of United States society in a 'post-9/11' era. (para. 7)

Not all post-9/11 films may reflect American culture. This implied that a post-9/11 film is similar to what defines an American working modern myth. Myths have provided guidance to people in need.

Jung (2010) suggested that post-9/11 films are a spectacle of real life images with narratives mixed with terrorist violence.

> They distinctly refer to real violence, inserting referential images or narrative, they respond [to] the political fall-out of 9/11 by engaging with the U.S. response, both on the level of narrative and cinematic narration. Without introducing a watershed 'Grand Theory' through the backdoor, such a combination constitutes a narrative challenge. (p. 16)

Post-9/11 films are modern myths that utilize narrative and cinematic narration to display referential images/narrative, terrorist violence and the U.S. response of political fall-out of the actual 9/11. They do not offer a "cure-all" solution to the 9/11 fallout, but offer to engage the viewers on their response to the events. At the end of *The Dark Knight*, Batman sacrificed his reputation and became vilified in the eyes of the citizens of Gotham City. The film concluded with an uncertain future for Gotham City and Batman.

Terrorism. According to Black (2004), terrorists are individuals who use force to demand a return to a previous social order. "Terrorism commonly begins as a form of coercion-a threat backed by force… terrorists typically demand a restoration of the past, such as political independence, lost territory, or a customary way of life" (p. 18). In *Batman Begins* and *The Dark Knight* Batman is fighting crime to return Gotham City to the state that he remembers as a child while *The Dark Knight* Joker fights to return Gotham to what it was like before Batman.

Terrorists often recruit others secretly with no real designated leader, just a meeting point and instructions on what the individual needs to do. Jones (2008) explained this "leaderless group" as something that modern terrorists do. "Contemporary terrorism is more likely the result of rapidly evolving 'leaderless groups' or 'self-starters' in which there is little overt recruitment" (p. 7). These are individual terrorist cells which might not know who they are working for and may never meet their employer. *The Dark Knight* began with the Joker hiring men to rob a bank. These individuals have never met each other, nor have they met the Joker.

Black (2004) believed that a war against terrorists is classified as an unconventional war and explains further aspects that define terrorism like: using very dangerous weapons, civilians are commonly targeted instead of military because terrorists prefer to strike civilians in urban settings due to the high amounts of potential targets and the terrorists can blend in with the urban crowds. While terrorism may look like war, there is a lack of what Black referred to as "game-like elements". These elements are uniforms, mercy to surrendering units, a defined beginning and conclusion. Most importantly following a war's conclusion both sides may become friends again. Due to the lack of game-like elements, fighting against terrorists is not the same as a standard war between cities or nations because once a standard war has ended, Black insisted that terrorism must not be taken as guerrilla warfare, which favors "inaccessible rural" locations. Terrorists never stop; they are a relentless force that does not stop until it has succeeded. Terrorism is not "ordinary crime" and therefore terrorists and their activities should not be treated like ordinary criminals or crimes. They should be dealt with on a higher level. If a terrorist is captured the terrorist will also wait for another chance for future attacks. Black (2004) implied that terrorism is more than crime but it is also not war.

> Terrorism is highly moralistic, however, it belongs to the same family as law and other social control. It differs from ordinary crime in other respects as well, such as its highly organized and war-like character. To classify terrorism merely as a form of crime thus obscures its sociological identity and obstructs its scientific understanding. (p. 16 - 17)

Black (2004) suggested that terrorists take their fight into the civilian world where the endgame in a terrorist's mind is win or die, negotiation is never an option. Terrorists often target highly populated civilian urban areas. In these largely populated areas terrorists are surrounded by potential targets or the terrorists may blend into the crowds. Terrorism is beyond an ordinary crime and to consider it on a lower level ruins the understanding of terrorism. Nolan's Joker had a unique ability to blend into the crowds. Several times during *The Dark Knight* the Joker remained undetected and continued to hide among Gotham City until he was ready to strike. Nolan's Joker also targeted public buildings and figures, not military targets.

Mayerfeld (2008) stated that America's involvement in the overthrow of Saddam Hussein were the actions of a terrorist nation. In this incident, America invaded Iraq, overthrew Saddam Hussein and killed innocents.

> In March 2003 the United States invaded Iraq. By the time US troops seized Baghdad and overthrew Saddam Hussein in early April, they had killed many thousand civilians. Like the worst terrorists, the war's architects, planners, and executors claimed that their cause was just. (p. 119)

However, Mayerfeld's (2008) statement goes against Black's "game-like elements" and Jones's (2008) "[terrorist] leaderless groups." While the actions may seem terroristic, America did have many game-like elements. This classifies America as a war nation instead of terrorist nation. Nolan's Batman may have acted like a terrorist. However, Nolan's Batman had game-like elements like a uniform and a clear end to his fight against crime. While Nolan's Batman targeted civilians he only targeted criminals.

Terrorism can be seen as a type of communication. Tuman (2010) believed that there is a connection between terrorism and communication and defined the concept of terrorism as a "threat-and violence-based communication processes" (p. 24). Terrorism communicates with large scale spectacles that send messages to their immediate targets and the world. A terrorist makes a threat and if the demand is not met, the terrorist follows through on the threat. *The Dark Knight's* Joker made constant threats that were not met and the consequence was death or destruction.

Osama bin Laden. America was at war with terrorists and the nation wanted to get the terrorist who claimed responsibility for the devastation of 9/11, Osama bin Laden. Gathering information on the whereabouts of bin Laden was very difficult because bin Laden was used to living on the run. According to Kagan and Kagan (2011) bin Laden was an expert in concealed movement and utilizing established communications in his terrorist network.

> It has taken 10 years to find and attack Osama bin Laden because of the inherent difficulty of getting actionable intelligence on a single individual who is well-versed in the arts of concealed movement, operational security, and the careful and disciplined use of electronic means of communication. In other words, it is generally very hard to find and act against senior and experienced terrorist leaders. (Kagan & Kagan, 2011, para. 1)

The difficulty in finding bin Laden was due to the fact that he was an experienced terrorist leader who the US was not familiar in dealing with. *The Dark Knight's* Batman had difficulty finding the Joker. The Joker was an expert in concealment, which he utilized to enter and escape the areas of his public targets. *The Dark Knight's* Alfred, butler and guardian of the younger Bruce Wayne, suggested that Wayne was wrong in dealing with the Joker as a common criminal.

Counterterrorism. According to Black (2004), agents of counterterrorism try to preemptively plan against terrorists. Some of the tactics they use can also include torture to further information gathering.

> Counterterrorism is primarily preventive, even preemptive, striking and possibly killing terrorists before they themselves can strike... It looks to the future-to what might happen where-guarding potential targets, screening for bombs and other weapons... It likewise employs various intelligence techniques (possibly including torture) to locate terrorists before they can launch attacks. (p. 23)

Counterterrorism agents need to understand terrorists to the point of predicting what their future targets will be, in order to effectively stop them. *The Dark Knight* Batman could not always stop the Joker because Batman considered the Joker to be just a common criminal.

The coalition forces in the war against terror experienced great difficulty in setting up a "targeted strike" on Osama bin Laden due to bin Laden's experience in the arts of blending, concealment and constant movement. According to Kagan & Kagan (2011) orchestrating a large scale attack on bin Laden was difficult because the operation was very time sensitive.

> Capturing or killing a high-value leader through a targeted strike requires knowing where that individual will be at a particular place and time in the future... The difficulty of knowing not where someone is, but where he will be when the strike force arrives, makes targeted strikes very difficult. (Kagan & Kagan, 2011, para. 2)

The Dark Knight Batman could not anticipate the Joker's next move or target. Batman had to rely on investigating what the Joker left behind, then attempt to stop him. However according to Black (2004), terrorism spawns counterterrorism. Counterterrorism is a downward spiral that is much more lethal than its enemy terrorism.

> Terrorism begets counterterrorism, a case of the social control of social control: justice in response to crime that is itself a form of justice. Terrorism is a particularly aggressive form of justice, and so is its social control. Counterterrorism is considerably more aggressive than ordinary criminal justice-partly warfare and partly law. (p. 22)

Because counterterrorism needs to anticipate terrorism, counterterrorism is more dangerous and as stated above, a prolonged engagement might elevate counterterrorism to disastrous levels. *The Dark Knight* Batman was a product of increased violence and Batman had to resort to physical torture. When the Joker was captured he revealed that bombs were going to kill Harvey Dent and Rachel Dawes. Batman tortured the Joker in order to gain the locations of Dent and Dawes, but it was ineffective. The Joker ended up telling Batman and the police where to find them because it was a game to the Joker. *The Dark Knight* also had Batman torture a mob boss by throwing him off the side of a building.

THE P.A.T.R.I.O.T. ACT

Post-9/11 had America declaring a "War on Terror", America was fighting abroad while trying to secure the home front from further domestic terrorism. The "P.A.T.R.I.O.T. Act" was established with a particular note of "Act 1" which increased the use of surveillance. According to Scheppele (2004), the increase allowed the Government greater use of electronic surveillance on citizens as an instrument for gathering intelligence. "[With the USA PATRIOT Act] the government need only assert that 'a significant purpose' of the requested surveillance is national security. This implies that there may be other purposes for surveillance, such as gathering information for criminal investigations" (p. 35). While America increased the amount of security to ensure safety, the increase came at a loss of some citizens' freedom. The character Batman would constantly scale buildings and observe Gotham City in an effort to stop crime. Batman could be anywhere at any time and the comic Batman would have hidden cameras scattered around Gotham City, constantly monitoring for criminals and villains who might threaten Gotham City.

Simone (2009) pointed out that citizens could be subjected to roving surveillance without consent.

> [The PATRIOT Act] allows the government to adhere to less stringent standards for search and seizure, thus permitting more surveillance activities to occur without public scrutiny… Furthermore, this provision could subject innocent citizens

to roving surveillance without their knowledge or expressed consent. (p. 3)

When government officials passed the PATRIOT Act they took away citizens' rights of privacy by allowing government agencies the option of subjecting all domestic American citizens to un-consented roving surveillance. *The Dark Knight* had Batman use a computer that hacked into Gotham City citizens' mobile phones. This was an advanced form of wiretapping, which mapped out the phones' immediate areas. Batman's wiretapping also scanned every phone in order to find the location of the Joker.

Immediately following 9/11, increased surveillance domestically was a large concern. According to Ip (2011) *The Dark Knight* had its connections with a counter surveillance system that was run by the National Security Agency. The system was implemented as part of America's increased security in order to help locate potential domestic terrorists. Ip argued that this reference was more of a critique instead of an approval of real life situations. "For various reasons the film's depiction of controversial counterterrorism measures is better seen as a critique rather than as an approval of the Bush Administration's war on terrorism" (p. 229). While Ip (2009) had reservations about the interpreted meaning between *The Dark Knight* and real world policies, a connection between *The Dark Knight* and post-9/11counter surveillance is implied. *The Dark Knight* and post-9/11 events suggests that *The Dark Knight* is a modern myth.

Color-Coded System. Following the 9/11 terrorist attacks on America, the US Government increased the issue of public safety. A color-coded system of warning was enacted. This warning was to inform everyone how severe the risk the immediate area was potentially in. According to Paul and Park (2002), the rationale behind this system was to establish a level of control in a time of terrorist chaos and communicate threats to the public. But the system was flawed and could potentially be misused.

> In response to 9/11, and in line with the department's created purpose, the DHS designed a color-coded system of warning (the Homeland Security Advisory System) that would 'create a

> common vocabulary, context, and structure' to communicate threats to the American public and offer knowledge of how to respond to said threats... [However] there is no independent evaluation of the legitimacy of a named threat, the system becomes vulnerable to manipulation by government officials for symbolic purposes. (p. 8)

This warning system was an indicator, allowing citizens the option of preparing for a possible attack. The warning system color status was based on current information gathered by America's intelligence agencies. In Nolan's *The Dark Knight* Police Captain James Gordon used the Bat signal in a similar way. While there was no immediate threat that the police needed Batman for, Gordon was using the signal as a reminder to the citizens of Gotham that Batman was somewhere in the city.

Fear and Loss of Control. Another aspect of post-9/11 culture was the growth of fear. After the initial shock from the attack on 9/11 many citizens felt vulnerable. While discussing the film *V for Vendetta* Jung (2010) stated that 9/11 also caused a cultural shift to paranoia and fear.

> Another way in which the film refers to collective anxieties and confusions in the contemporary climate is the motif of paranoia and conspiracy. Dixon attests a general state of paranoia and fear in post-9/11 America which was expressed in cultural products such as cinema. (p. 80)

The extent to which fear and paranoia is utilized in a film is another aspect of a post-9/11 film. The Nolan Batman utilized fear and conspiracy as central plot devices for *Batman Begins* and *The Dark Knight*.

Batman Begins established Bruce Wayne who was training himself. However, The League of Shadows taught him that his greatest weapon is the use of fear. Wayne returned to Gotham and created the symbol of Batman. The League of Shadows regrouped and followed Wayne back to Gotham City where the league was planning on releasing a fear toxin to spread fear into the citizens of Gotham which would cause the citizens to turn on each other and possibly burn down the city.

Batman continued using fear i*n The Dark Knight*; while James Gordon used the Bat Signal as a device of fear to keep the city in order. The end of *The Dark Knight* revealed a conspiracy being forged between James Gordon and Batman in order to stop the Joker's plans and maintain peace in Gotham City.

The Media. The events of 9/11 were felt first hand by those in the respective areas that were attacked. But most of the world experienced it through media. Jung (2010) wrote, due to its lack of censorship, democratic news media (non-government controlled) is part of 9/11 because it allowed most of us to experienced 9/11 virtually.

> The visual media itself is part of the "event 9/11", first of all, because most Americans (and many others) experienced the event on television, yet felt personally assaulted and threatened. Therefore, this second-hand vicariously-lived element is an important part of the way in which we try to grasp the event 9/11. (p. 54)

Democratic media is part of 9/11 and it continues to be a critical element in a post-9/11 world.

Effective terrorists quickly understood the value of media in helping them get their messages across. According to Tuman (2010), terrorists sought out reporters and quickly became as accommodating as possible.

> Terrorist groups also learned that manipulation of media could be achieved if they approached news reporters acting less like terrorists and more like politicians or public relations experts… By granting interviews to some but not all reporters as individuals, or newspapers or television networks as entities, terrorists could hold out the promise of a competitive scoop while also guaranteeing coverage. (p. 197)

Terrorism and media share an interesting relationship because of sensational news. Effective terrorism needs the media to spread their message and the media needs terrorism to boost their ratings. In *The Dark Knight* the Joker kidnapped a reporter and his camera person. The Joker made the reporter read the Joker's demands to Gotham City.

In order for the immediate terrorist message to get communicated, the terrorist needs to focus on attracting news media. Supporting this, Jung (2010) recorded that media reporting can be very effective. Terrorists could begin spreading fear and panic to others outside their immediate region.

> Media reporting can help the enemy – here, help the terrorists to send a message to the world, a symbiosis between terrorist and the mass media – is an influential one. For if the end goal of terrorists is to spread fear and panic far beyond their immediate victims, they need media coverage for impact, to gain the maximum potential leverage needed to effect fundamental political change. (Jung, 2010, p. 60)

The larger a group that can be reached, the great potential the terrorist group has of others supporting their goals. A successful large scale act of terror creates a ripple effect which gets the attention of many people.

Tuman (2010) pointed out that there are many groups of "audiences" who are affected when terrorist strike. These groups include governments and institutional officials, the public as well as others.

> Government officials (if a state policy is implicated in the message) or institutional officials (if an organizational or institutional policy or practice is implicated in the message) will serve as a distinct but potentially overlapping target audience. The public audience will often be used (as suggested before) to leverage pressure against the government or institutional audience to change a policy or practice to comply with the terrorist's demands. (p. 34)

Many different audiences become involved with a successful large scale terrorist attack. This could work in the favor of the terrorist who may seek a change in social policy. *The Dark Knight's* Joker would appear on television and make demands. In his message to Gotham City, the Joker was aware that he was also talking to public officials.

GENRE ANALYSIS: THE GANGSTER, THE EVOLVED DETECTIVE, AND THE DARK KNIGHT

As the cycle between terrorism and the media continue, the demand for a greater terroristic spectacle is also raised. Jung (2010) recorded that terrorists need to plan something big and spectacular in order to become credible.

> Terrorism is a media savvy, staged act. Terrorist events are choreographed to attract media and press attention. The successful terrorist act must be spectacular, out of the ordinary, commanding and channeling worldwide attention. The media plays an important part in terrorism – in constructing perception of a conflict, and the legitimacy of its participant. (p. 60)

Terrorists are constantly adapting to further their cause actively including the media is good, but terrorists need to do something drastic to get the media interested in hearing the terrorists' message.

On this point Tuman (2010) stated that the desire for sensational news creates a fickle media and the result is an escalation on the side of terrorists, who need to devise larger and grander attacks to capture the eye of the media.

> In a world with media saturation, and news stories already devoted to coverage of so many issues relating to violence, death, and tragedy, guaranteeing coverage of a terrorism story requires visually compelling, dramatic, and therefore devastating violence on a larger and larger scale… if you kidnap three missionaries in the Philippines and demand that the government release rebel leaders, you might get a print news story and some local coverage. If you detonate a bomb at an embassy or in a public market, killing hundreds and injuring more, you will get more attention from print and broadcast news media. (p. 196)

Terrorists need to plan larger scaled attacks in order for media to become interested in the terrorists' message. *The Dark Knight's* Joker kept escalating his targets. The Joker began his public threats by killing public officials. He then escalated to a hospital if a public accountant was not killed; this threat caused panic in the streets of Gotham City. His final threat was to leave the city before nightfall, those that do not will deal with the Joker.

To this point it may be implied that our desire for news and the media's desire for ratings, encourage terrorism. Jung (2010) found that the demand of sensational news pushes terrorists to larger targets and heists. "If terrorism is theatre, we are its audience, and if terrorism relies on the media, we are implicated through the demand of sensational news" (p. 83). The media is a gatekeeper for terrorists getting their message to the world. The media is a friend to the public for not reporting what it deems "low-end" terrorist attacks and the public's enemy for coaxing the terrorists to take action. Due to this it is only a matter of time before the terrorists unleash an attack of large enough magnitude for the media's delight to report and the public's horror to virtually experience.

Videotaped Messages. Videotaped messages are an important aspect to consider when discussing 9/11. Terrorists relied on these to send a message to America commonly including current events. Osama Bin Laden made a videotape which mentioned the upcoming election between Kerry and Bush. Bin Laden was also attempting to convince the American public that they were the real people who determined their own security, not the president. As the FOX News website reported, "[bin Laden said] Your security is not in the hands of Kerry, Bush or Al Qaeda. Your security is in your own hands,'… 'Any state that does not mess with our security, has naturally guaranteed its own security'" (FoxNews.com, 2004, para. 4). *The Dark Knight's* Joker made a videotape to be aired on the nightly news. In the video the Joker pleaded with the citizens of Gotham City to try to convince them that Batman made the city crazy. The Joker attempted to get the citizens on his side to stop Batman and make Batman's true identity known.

Terrorists incorporated different tactics to dishearten and force a military withdrawal of American soldiers from the war. During post-9/11 the public witnessed terrorists recording the beheading of Americans and posting the uncensored videos online. Public mutilation of bodies was an effective tool that America's enemies used in previous conflicts. Costigan (2007) stated that beheadings and other disturbing images have proven effective in changing foreign policy, including an incident in Somalia which shown mutilated American soldiers. "Musab al-Zarqawi undoubtedly realized this, and may well have been the jihadis' leading proponent of webcasting when he posted video of the beheading of the American contractor Nicholas Berg on 11 May 2004 on the website of *Muntada al Ansar al-Islami*" (p. 13-14). Disturbing images are common in a post-9/11 world. In *The Dark Knight* one of the Joker's videotapes to the news, included a "Batman Copycat" being humiliated by the Joker. At the end of the videotape, it is implied that the Joker was killing the Batman Copycat. Earlier in *The Dark Knight*, the dead body of the tormented "Batman Copycat" was found hanged off the side of City Hall.

To a certain extent acts of terrorism may be seen as art. According to Jung (2010), the comparison between art and demolition were linked by the destruction of the Twin Towers. Jung mentioned that the whole point of terrorism is to produce an emotional response similar to art.

> Karl Heinz Stockhausen… described the demolition of the Twin Towers as 'a work of art'… Terrorism – and this includes spectacularly publicized events such as 11 September as well as videoed executions – has always needed an audience. Bomb blasts on symbolic targets and killings on camera are dramatic productions designed to elicit an emotional response – just like theatre. (p. 53)

While a very drastic degree of expressionism, an audience is required for both art and terrorism. *The Dark Knight* Joker blew up a hospital, that fell with a controlled explosion. The Joker addressed sociological issues to the citizens of Gotham City and the movie audience. These sociological issues were Batman's presence, if Gotham City still needed him, and how governments attempted to provide a false sense of control through an implied plan. The Joker also used variations of sociological experements "The Ticking Bomb Scenario" as well as "The Prisoner's Dilemma."

Torture and the Ticking Bomb Scenario. The "ticking bomb scenario" presents a situation that might justify the use of torture on a suspect. Mayerfeld (2008) wrote the scenario involves a bomb in an unknown location that will explode killing innocents. The individual who planted the bomb was apprehended but refuses to disclose where the bomb is. If torture is the only way the individual will divulge the bomb's location and save lives, does this justify torturing the bomber?

> A bomb has been planted that, if allowed to explode, will kill some number of innocent civilians… The man who planted the bomb has fallen into our custody, and refuses to tell us its location. If torturing the man is the only way for us to locate and defuse the bomb, thereby saving innocent people's lives, then aren't we morally permitted—even required—to torture him? This shows that torture is sometimes justified as a means of preventing terrorism'… It is the main justification for the use of torture by the US government in the 'War on Terror'. (p. 110)

Does the ticking bomb scenario justify the use of torture on enemy suspects? Accurate information is vital when dealing with terrorists, and torture is often used to gain it.

According to Allhoff (2003) the use of torture is illegal in America and no government agency can legally practice torture abroad. Instead of breaking policy directly, America outsourced torture by hiring foreign countries.

> American officials have admitted that the United States has transferred prisoners to the intelligence agencies of Jordan, Egypt, and/or Morocco, all of which are known for using torture as a method of interrogation. Reportedly, some of these prisoners have even been handed over along with lists of questions to which they might know the answers and whose answers would be valuable to the United States. (Allhoff, 2003, p. 105)

One may imply that this backdoor tactic of keeping American officials from breaching policy is proof that America does support torture. *The Dark Knight* Batman interrogated the Joker in a police holding cell. During the interrogation, Batman physically tortured the Joker in order to gain information to save the Joker's hostages. During this scene, James Gordon and his police force observed the torture in a separate room.

The information gathered in the torture of terrorists proved fruitful in discovering the location of bin Laden. Shane & Savage (2011) stated that "enhanced interrogation techniques" are what led the US to capture bin Laden. "As intelligence officials disclosed the trail of evidence that led to the compound in Pakistan where [bin] Laden was hiding, a chorus of Bush administration officials claimed vindication for their policy of 'enhanced interrogation techniques'" (para. 2). This real world application suggested that torture was a useful tool in capturing the elusive bin Laden.

While there may be people who criticize torture, Klavan (2008) pointed out that people are usually just interested in results and keeping clean. When things get dirty, we are more apt to turn our backs on them even if their job is a necessity.

> When heroes arise who take those difficult duties on themselves, it is tempting for the rest of us to turn our backs on them, to vilify them in order to protect our own appearance of righteousness. We prosecute and execrate the violent soldier or the cruel interrogator in order to parade ourselves as paragons of the peaceful values they preserve. (Klavan, 2008, para. 13)

Klavan (2008) believed that torture is a necessary evil. While we do not agree with the practice of torture, it possibly provides useful information that could save lives.

Allhoff (2003) suggested that when dealing with the torture of terrorists, most should consider the rights of the many out weighting the rights of the few. Allhoff stated that it is justified to violate the bombers' rights to not be tortured in order to save the potential innocent victims who could be violated or killed unjustly.

> This [shows] that there can be cases involving rights conflicts where one right has to be violated in order to prevent further rights from being violated... By violating his right not to be tortured, we can therefore ensure that the innocents' rights to not be killed unjustly are not violated. (p.109)

The Batman character is a vigilante hero who is allowed to act violently toward criminals. *The Dark Knight* Batman tortured the Joker in order to find the location of innocent civilian Rachel Dawes.

Arguments Against Torture. Misinformation is a great concern when dealing with torturing a suspect. Mayerfeld (2008) stated that the risk is too great to even consider torture as a viable tool because the information gathered could be false and might lead to a greater disaster. "Consider the problem of false information, which not only causes delays, swallows man hours, and leads down blind alleys, but can also encourage disastrous choices" (p. 111). Mayerfeld (2008) presented a strong case against torture because the risk of generating false information is too great and could potentially cost more manpower and lives.

Ip (2011) mocked the ticking bomb scenario but pointed out the ineffectiveness of torture by applying it to various scenes of *The Dark Knight*. Ip stated that throughout the film torture was used and it was ineffective.

> The use of torture and coercion in *The Dark Knight* is uniformly ineffective... [Batman] tried—also unsuccessfully—to obtain a lead on the Joker's whereabouts by questioning mobster Sal Maroni... the Joker reveals the location of Dent and Dawes. However, he does this not because Batman's physical torture has broken him but because he wishes to make Batman choose whom to rescue... *The Dark Knight's* depiction of the effectiveness of torture and coercive interrogation is therefore skeptical. (p. 220)

Ip (2008) brought up good points about the ticking bomb scenario and the ineffectiveness of torture in real life as well as in *The Dark Knight*. It should be noted that the issue seemed to stand as a testament toward the Joker as something beyond your standard criminal. *The Dark Knight* Joker was not a common criminal. Alfred warned Bruce Wayne not to assume that the Joker was a standard criminal. Wayne did treat the Joker as a regular criminal, which aided in the Joker rising to power over the mobs and Gotham City.

The Joker was a terrorist and belonged on a level higher than criminals but lower than war-level.

Jung (2010) wrote that in accordance with "Just War Theory" and the writings of Khatchadourian that we must all strive to be a "moral being." "Instead of a categorical right to life, Khatchadourian postulates one supreme human right, the right to be treated as a 'moral being' not as a thing or object. This right cannot be overridden or waived; it is inalienable" (p. 62). Jung (2010) insists that maintaining moral standards in the face of adversity is vital.

But what if we encounter someone who has tortured others, did not care about becoming a "moral being", and was in the process of doing great moral horror? As a counter Allhoff (2003) stated that Robert Nozick was always against the violation of rights. Nozick believed in "side constraints": that under no circumstance is anyone allowed to minimize the rights of the other. However, Allhoff pointed out that Nozick did not apply his beliefs to large scale catastrophes.

> [Nozick] conceives as rights of 'side constraints,' which is to say that rights are absolute and inviolable; no considerations or circumstances can warrant intentional assault on anyone's rights, regardless of the end being pursued (including minimization of rights violations overall)… Nozick, in a footnote, admits that it is an open question whether these side constraints are 'absolute or may be violated in order to avoid catastrophic moral horror.' (p. 109-110)

Allhoff (2003) implied that Nozick did not go on record that side constraints were still valid to possibly avoid a large scale moral horror.

THE JOKER AS A TERRORIST

Vilifying a group is a tactic that is commonly used to draw people together. According to Tuman (2010) this has been done since the Greeks and is when a group is trying to band together against another group. The opposition is labeled as "the Other".

> Ideological hegemony and privileging of one culture over another can certainly be observed where people within a dominant culture create a sense of shared identity dependent on the construction of a counterpoint-an outsider group or culture that becomes a point of comparison and a rationalizing mechanism for hegemony. We call this [out-group] *the Other*. (p. 58)

During post-9/11 "the Other" were Muslims.

Following 9/11 Muslims were "the Other". However, Jung (2010) stated that there was another "Other" that emerged. Modern cinema developed an enemy known as "terrorist other." The terrorist other is either alien or if they are domestic, then they are mentally disturbed. "In the typical terrorist action movie, the terrorists are depicted as an alien 'other'. If the terrorist is homegrown, he is usually disturbed or psychotic" (Jung, 2010, p.45). It was implied that The Dark Knight Joker was American and psychotic.

Rodriguez (2010) believed that *The Dark Knight* Joker was not only disturbed but madness incarnate, "The Joker, like madness itself, cannot be annihilated but he can be isolated, diagnosed and compelled to enter a therapeutic discourse" (p. 17). *The Dark Knight* Batman believed that the Joker could still be understood. However, Alfred advised Bruce Wayne that some men cannot be understood.

Camp, Webster, Coverdale, and Nairn (2010) did an exercise where they psychologically analyzed the Joker and found a number of aspects that categorize the Joker as insane. These traits include his appearance, clothes, use of language, mannerisms and behavior.

> The Joker's depiction as not normal or human further enhances this constructed madness by synergies between the use of language, appearance, behavior, and intertextual elements including mad dogs and "The Screaming Pope." ... Suggestive behavior includes laughing when threatened with death, being unconstrained by social rules and expectations, cavalierly disregarding the consequences of his behavior, absence of fear, and destructive, animalistic actions. His

actions show him as beyond social controls in seeking his own malignant ends... there are hints of earlier incarnations of the Joker as a hugely damaged being from DC Comics and the earlier film *Batman*... Taken together, the "mad dog" and "not normal" aspects of the portrayal strongly imply that the Joker is mad. (Camp et al., 2010, p. 148)

The psychological assessment clearly displayed that *The Dark Knight* Joker is "mad" and fits the definition of a post-9/11 "psychotic terrorist other."

Kolenic (2009) stated that *The Dark Knight* Joker's messages actually go deeper than they seem. Kolenic suggested that the Joker is not mad but actually on a crusade to show the citizens of Gotham that their world of control is just an illusion.

> The [Joker] taps into something the audience cannot completely write off... It is this danger—this attraction to the chaos [Joker] represents—that institutions temper, control, segment, and attempt to defuse. Institutions, in this calibration, refer to schools, churches, governmental authorities ... These institutions—and governance in general—give their subjects both real and necessarily unreal senses of order, control... When these institutions are breeched... It gives access to the living contemporary webs of meaning and cultural anxieties. (p. 1024-1025)

While the Joker may seem like he is crazy and out of control. Kolenic's (2001) view is *The Dark Knight* Joker resembled the archetype of "the fool," who on the surface is comical, but speaks the truth. *The Dark Knight* Joker was constantly urging the citizens of Gotham City to see past the unrealistic sense of security that Batman and the police were building up. This philosophy was adopted by *The Dark Knight* Harvey Dent who went on a vengeful killing spree as "Two-Face."

Creating Followers. *The Dark Knight* Joker attempted to convince people to see things his way. According to Jones (2008), individuals need to be connected to something larger.

> Conversion involves a transformation of the self and that it connects the individual to something considered sacred, ie., something that functions to connect the individual to something greater than their own ego and give them a sense of meaning and purpose and a source of values to live by. (p. 5)

Converts need some type of inspiration to live by. During Nolan's *Batman Begins* and *The Dark Knight*, Bruce Wayne was trying to take a stand against organized crime in Gotham City. During *Batman Begins*, Wayne underwent training with a group known as "The League of Shadows." The league taught Wayne the fundamentals of how to control and use fear as a weapon. Wayne left the group to return to Gotham City with a clear mission. Wayne created the identity known as "Batman" as a symbol against crime and for the citizens of Gotham City to rally behind to reclaim their city. This concept was expanded in *The Dark Knight* where untrained citizens were dressing up like Batman and attempting to stop crime. This response was not what Wayne had in mind when he first created Batman. *The Dark Knight* also had the Joker, who was a murderous vigilante who went against public officials instead of criminals.

Zinnbauer & Pargament (1998) found that converts are more susceptible during hardship. "[a convert is] actively seeking the conversion experience to resolve life difficulties" (p. 162). When faced with crisis people are most vulnerable for conversions. *The Dark Knight* Joker attempted to convince the citizens of Gotham City that Batman was the cause of Gotham City's turmoil of civil unrest. This unrest was of people endangering themselves by becoming vigilantes and the city needing to resort to a vigilante in order to correct itself. In order to stop the craziness of Batman, the Joker began a killing spree; for each day that Batman did not reveal who he really was, the Joker killed someone. Instead of killing civilians, the Joker's targets were public officials. When a city must resort to the aid of a vigilante, it may be interpreted that the law and public officials are ineffective in their positions. The killing of public officials also increased the unrest and strife with the citizens of Gotham City. As *The Dark Knight* progressed, the Joker's attacks grew which may have caused more uneasiness with the citizens of Gotham City as the Joker continued his pleas to get the citizens to share his view of the world. During *The Dark Knight* Harvey Dent's great loss and hardship came from being physically altered and losing his fiancée, Rachel Dawes. The Joker convinced Dent to adopt the Joker's philosophy on life. This caused Dent to become "Two-Face" and begin his own killing spree of vengeance.

THE PRISONER'S DILEMMA

A social experiment that should be understood for this paper is "The Prisoner's Dilemma." Ashmore (1987) stated that this game theory encourages the benefits of cooperation versus competition.

> Advocate using the game to assist in simulating such concepts as interdependence, structure, power, and trust. The game can be used in any unit which has the principles of negotiation as a focus, or in a course which has a unit on rationalism, game theory, cooperation vs. competition, or even the concept of social reality. Participating in the simulation allows the student to experience and therefore operationalize such concepts as real and perceived conflict, power, moral victory, and interdependence. (p. 117-118)

The Prisoner's Dilemma can be applied to a number of fields where individuals can observe various social aspects as well as power and trust.

How The Prisoner's Dilemma works is explained by Chojnacki (2004) who added that the game typically involves two players who must choose between "cooperation" and "defection." Their outcome is between individual rationality versus group rationality.

> [The Prisoner's Dilemma] exemplifies the friction between individual and group interests. Previous research on [The Prisoner's Dilemma] has focused on cooperation by individuals, and how it is, or fails to be, achieved… The original [Prisoner's Dilemma] situation allowed for only two players, each of who can choose between two actions, typically called cooperation and defection. The [Prisoner's Dilemma] embodies the tension between individual rationality (reflected in the incentive of both sides to be selfish) and

group rationality (reflected in the higher payoff to both sides for mutual cooperation over mutual defection)... The outcome in the [Prisoner's Dilemma] is defined as the result of the players' decisions. (p. 6)

The Dark Knight Joker ran a social experiment on the citizens of Gotham City. The Joker's experiment had two transportation ferries: one with citizens the other with convicted criminals. Each was loaded with explosives and held the other's detonator. The Joker demanded that one blow up the other before midnight, or he would blow both of the boats up.

The game is set up to display individualism and group dynamics. The final verdict is determined by the choices made by the individuals. Reboul (2006) provided a full outline of every possible outcome complete with rewards and penalties.

> The Prisoner's Dilemma is a non-null sum game, which is played by two or more players. The rule is extremely simple: in each run, each player has two simple options: either cooperate or defect. The gain is calculated on the basis of what both players choose to do, as shown on the table below:

	Options	1st Player	
2nd Player		Cooperate	Defect
	Cooperate	1st = 3; 2nd = 3	1st = 5; 2nd = 0
	Defect	1st = 0; 2nd = 5	1st = 1; 2nd = 1

> At first glance, it seems that the moral of the Prisoner's Dilemma is the archetype uncooperative behavior: defection. If you defect, at worst, you will win 1 point and at best 5, while if you cooperate, at worst you will win nothing, while at best you will win 3 points. This seems an incentive not to cooperate, but the main contribution of Axelrod and his colleagues was to show that, in fact, defecting is a sure path to defeat. (p. 478)

The Prisoner's Dilemma displayed the reward of mutual cooperation.

The Dark Knight ferry scene had citizens struggle between trusting that the inmates would not blow up the citizens' boat and should the citizens blow up the inmates' boat in order to survive. This was solved by none of the citizens having the heart to physically activate the detonator that would blow up the inmates' boat. While both of the ferries survived by not blowing each other up; Batman stopped the Joker from blowing up both of the boats.

"Can We Eliminate Evil?" (2012), stated that humans have evolved to understand the benefits of mutual cooperation,

> Are people getting nicer because they're getting smarter and believe it or not the answer is maybe yes. IQ scores have been increasing throughout the 20th century and all over the world… But as a result it's not farfetched to think that people could see the benefits of cooperation and see the downsides of violence more as they start to intellectualize their lives. (time code. 40:59)

This episode suggested that humans might be genetically coded toward cooperation. In *The Dark Knight* both boats survived by cooperation and trust in each other. Batman did stop the Joker; however, if one of the boats blew up the other, it is unclear if the Joker would have kept his word and let the surviving boat go unexploded.

Ip (2011) observed that *The Dark Knight*'s Joker set up his own version of "The Prisoner's Dilemma." While this was Joker's social experiment it served as a reflection that people have a choice of how they should react to threats of terrorism.

> The Joker sets up a version of the prisoner's dilemma: either one ferry's passengers decide to blow up the other ferry along with its passengers, or the Joker blows up both ferries. The Joker's purpose in setting up this 'social experiment' is to demonstrate the capriciousness of modern civility… The film's message here is that even if the occurrence of terrorism is beyond control, people do have a measure of control over how they choose to respond to its occurrence. (Ip, 2011, p. 225)

Ip (2011) implies that terrorism can strike anywhere at any time, while it is very easy to lose ourselves in the madness, it is best to react calmly and accordingly because an irrational reaction is what the terrorists are hoping for.

METHODOLOGY

The method used for this paper will be "Generic Application" and "Semiotics." Foss (2004) explained that generic criticism is a fairly new method. Edwin Black was the first person to use the term in 1965. Generic criticism looks to find similarities between an artifact and rhetorical situations. Foss (2004) stated that the word "Genre" comes from the French term, "used to refer to a distinct group, type, class, or category of artifacts that share important characteristics that differentiate it from other groups" (p. 193). Generic application is the process in which an artifact is chosen and compared to a type of genre. The critic then compares the artifact to the genre and states if the artifact is a good or bad representation of the respective genre. Generic application needs two things, an artifact and a genre. The practice of semiotics was used in this paper to help establish the genre that the artifact will be compared to.

SEMIOTICS

Schatz (1981) explained "Semiotics" is as a science that studies human interaction and communication. He also credited Ferdinand de Saussure as the individual behind semiotics,

> Swiss linguist Ferdinand de Saussure, who suggested that language provides the 'master pattern' for the study of cultural signification. According to de Saussure, verbal language is the one sign system shared by all cultures; its basic structure informs every system of social communication. (p.19)

de Saussure implied that what a culture values can be seen in the culture's language. Certain film techniques such as the way a camera is framed to an actor, the editing cuts between shots and themes found in the film's storyline is a type of language used by the filmmakers to further express the message of the film.

de Saussure recognized the relationship between the signifier and the signified. Cobley and Jansz (1997) explained that de Saussure's "signifier" is a material aspect that when communicated, creates a mental concept known as "signified." Cobley and Jansz (1997) defined semiotics as, "a science that studies the life of signs within society… [Semiotics] would be a part of social psychology and consequently of general psychology" (p. 13). Society has a lot of signs which produce a meaning. A sign represents something that is trying to be expressed; this could be a thought, feeling, item, anything. Beginning with the host culture's language, is de Saussure's study of Semiotics.

Chandler (1994) explained the various aspects of semiotics and their importance. Chandler's work attempted to find the messages communicated through cultural aspects of signs, indexes, and signals. The study of semiotics attempts to discover if there are established codes that may exist within cultural artifacts and the effects of these messages on individuals.

> Semiotics offers the promise of a systematic, comprehensive and coherent study of communications phenomena as a whole, not just instances of it. Semiotics provides us with a potentially unifying conceptual framework and a set of methods and terms for use across the full range of signifying practices, which include gesture, posture, dress, writing, speech, photography, film, television and radio. (Chandler, 1994, p. 175)

Chandler (1994) implied that semiotics is similar to a language that once learned can be understood through various mediums of communication. It may be possible that certain semiotic methods and terms could mean the same thing across different cultures. As an example, the editing cuts, various lighting techniques, styles like film noir and most non-verbal gestures (semiotics) that are used in the production of a film might be understood by viewers from other cultures. An America film by an American director could be understood in another culture. Or a British director should be able to direct an American film and the semiotics of the film would be understood in a foreign country.

GENRES

Schatz (1981) pointed out that film genre is the product of the audience's repeat support of a certain narrative type. The narrative's success spawns more films of similar narrative and a film genre is developed. Schatz believed that this process explained how the film genres: Western, Gangster, Detective, etc. came to be. From here Schatz (1981) stated that the study of semiotics applied to film genre.

> A film genre, conversely, has come into being precisely because of its cultural significance as a meaningful narrative system. Whereas a verbal statement represents a speaker's organization of neutral components into a meaningful pattern, a genre film represents an effort to reorganize a familiar, meaningful system in an original way. (p. 19)

Using semiotics to understand film genre, it may be possible to decipher a unique language through film. The "Western genre" was about an individual who attempted to civilize the wild frontier. *The Dark Knight* Batman attempted to civilize the crime infested Gotham City. The "Gangster genre" had an individual who attempted to break away from social norms but was defeated by the city he tried to run. *The Dark Knight* Joker attempted to take over the city and suffered his first defeat by being refused by the citizens of Gotham City (the populace is a representation of the city) by not adopting his philosophies. The "Detective genre" had an individual who fought for the promise of a perfect world. *The Dark Knight* Batman fought crime in an attempt to return Gotham City to its previous glory. The "Evolved detective genre" threatened the safety of the hero and the hero was sometimes the ultimate victim. *The Dark Knight* concluded with Batman taking the blame for the Joker's work, this caused Batman to be chased down and hunted by the citizens and police of the city he tried to save.

Metz (2004) believed in de Saussure's work and developed "cinematographic grammar" which Metz believed could pass as a loose language. "The fact that must be understood is that films are understood. Iconic analogy alone cannot account for the intelligibility of the co-occurrences in filmic discourse" (p. 86). The images of film or the cinematography of film may be understood on a level beyond a standard icon. A film's cinematography might evoke an emotional reaction, feeling or thought from a foreign viewer regardless of cultural understanding.

Schatz (1981) wrote that films were calculated expressions of a filmmaker, a filmmaker who is from the audience or a "collective response." However, the success of a film genre depends on the approval of the audience. Schatz referred to "generic evolution" which is when the filmmaker and audience become more aware of the genre.

> A genre's variation tends to render both filmmakers and audience more sensitive to the form as distinct from its social function. This increasing sensitivity to a genre's formal make-up-to its rules of expression and composition-leads to a number of interesting developments as the genre evolves… But no matter how subversive or self-reflexive a genre film might appear to be, its success-like that of the genre-is necessarily a function of popular response. (p. 264)

With these aspects, it is implied that the collective audience determines what successful stories they would like to see again. The character of Batman might be seen as a product of a comic genre. The Batman comic book was originally a combination of other types of heroes that were created because of the success of Superman. During the 1940s, comic books were being turned into serials.

CONCLUSION

Myths may be seen as important to help a civilization with understanding and carrying on their culture. The mythos of the Batman universe spans generations. During this time, aspects of the Batman mythos as well as the character of Batman have been altered to fit the times. This may be due to the real world that influences the current creators of the Batman universe, or the creators deliberately altering the Batman universe to be accepted by the present audience. Myths are reflections of the myth's culture. The different iterations of the Batman universe might be seen as a reflection of that Batman universe's era.

CHAPTER 3
METHODOLOGY

The Dark Knight is a film directed by Christopher Nolan that was released in 2008. The film was a retelling of the superhero known as Batman and the universe that he resides in. While the film did make a lot of money and it was critically praised, this paper attempted to understand why Nolan decided to adopt his changes to the Batman universe. Using generic application, semiotics, and genre study, an understanding might be deciphered to from Nolan's choices and how a post-9/11 world may have caused such changes.

PURPOSE AND JUSTIFICATION

Foss's (2004), de Saussure's, and Schatz's (1981) classifications of "genre" were used to compare the relationship between text and the evolution of Batman's universe as seen in Christopher Nolan's 2008 film *The Dark Knight*. It was probably not the original intent of Foss, de Saussure and Schatz to have their paradigms directly connected to the film *The Dark Knight*. However, there is a harmony between generic application, semiotics, genre and how they may relate to *The Dark Knight* based on the genre model provided by Schatz through de Saussure's initial work. While the term genre might be loosely thrown around, Schatz's clear definitions of Western, Gangster and Evolved Detective can lock in specific aspects of films to give them a clear genre. *The Dark Knight* is a film that does not fit solely into one genre but into a couple of Schatz's genres. *The Dark Knight* Joker might be seen as a Gangster, *The Dark Knight* Batman's sacrifice at the end of the film may be seen as an Evolved Detective. *The Dark Knight* Batman struggles to bring order in a savage land. This implies elements of the Western genre. While these connections were made, these are not the only interpretations that might be made between *The Dark Knight* and these paradigms, others may be drawn with further research.

STUDY DESIGN

Christopher Nolan's film *The Dark Knight* was based on the comic book superhero known as Batman and Batman's universe. Nolan's *The Dark Knight* is also a film and not a comic book. This different medium provided the world a new version of the Batman mythos. Various sound and visual elements were utilized in order to successfully persuade the audience into feeling and thinking a certain way. Semiotics should be able to identify parallels between *The Dark Knight* and 9/11. It would be outside the scope of this paper to analyze all of the vast information spanning generations on the character of Batman and the Batman universe. The character Batman and the Batman universe continues to be altered, and produced on a weekly basis due to new comic books, television cartoons, video games and other media. This paper will examine eleven scenes from *The Dark Knight*.

This paper attempted to build upon other claims and introduce new comparisons. This paper is using the events of September 11, 2001 as a turning point in American culture, which may have affected Nolan's *The Dark Knight*. Certain September 11th and post-9/11 elements will be examined such as insurgent and terroristic activity: targeting financial institutions in daylight, public displaying of the enemy's dead mutilated bodies, distribution to the media of videotapes that contain messages, videotapes that contain executions of the enemy, terrorists' ability to blend into urban environments, the mixed signals of the P.A.T.R.I.O.T. Act, the use of fear mongering, the debate of torturing terrorist in order to gain information, and implying the symbolic connections of *The Dark Knight* Batman representing George W. Bush while *The Dark Knight* Joker represented Osama bin Laden.

These eleven scenes might help with the connection between *The Dark Knight* and 9/11. They might also help identify the established genres used by the filmmakers of *The Dark Knight*. The first scene is the first twelve minutes of *The Dark Knight*. This is important in setting the mood of the film and Gotham City. The film opened with silent production company logos. During this opening sequence we are introduced to the Joker and James Gordon and are offered a glimpse into how both of these characters operate. The Joker established himself as someone with little regard for established order by robbing a bank and killing his own men. His face paint and unusual behavior seem to identify him as an individual who is mentally unstable, which might explain his previous characteristics. As Vernet (1999) wrote, a silent opening scene might help identify the style of film noir present in the film. A following cut included James Gordon using the Bat Signal, a device used to contact Batman. However, Gordon does not need to contact Batman, instead he used the Bat Signal as a reminder to the city that Batman is out there. This action could be compared to the color-coded warning system.

The second is the hanged "Batman Copycat" with the Joker's videotaped message. The hanged solder and crudely made videotape might be seen as similar insurgent and terroristic behavior during the post-9/11 war in the Middle East. It might be compared with the writing of Costigan (2007) when talking about the use of beheadings and disturbing videotaped images in order to demand a change in social policy.

The third scene is Batman interrogating the Joker in the interrogation cell. The use of torture in order to save innocents was similar to the writings of Shane and Savage (2011) who stated that America used "enhanced interrogation techniques" in order to stop terrorists and save people. This scene also contained the Joker's variation of the "Ticking Bomb Scenario" which indirectly presented the audience with the difficulty of a moral decision and gave insight into the character of the Joker.

The fourth scene is Lucius Fox helping Batman locate the Joker with Batman's new sonar wiretapping. Comparisons between this scene and real life may be identified with the P.A.T.R.I.O.T. Act. As stated by Simone (2009), anyone could be unknowingly wiretapped at anytime. In real life and *The Dark Knight* wiretapping was utilized in order to locate domestic terrorist activity.

The fifth scene is the ferry boats that the Joker attempts to use to perform a "social experiment" between innocent citizens and prisoners of Gotham City.

The Joker performed a variation of the "Prisoner's Dilemma," one of the boats had to blow up the other before midnight or both would be blown up by the Joker. Once again the Joker indirectly presented the audience with a moral dilemma. However, the boats defy him and the boats of citizens which represent the city, cooperate against the Joker. Similar to the Schatz (1981) Gangster genre, the gangster (Joker) is defeated at the hands of the city.

The sixth scene is the last few minutes of *The Dark Knight*, during this time it looked like the Joker was going to win by ruining all the legal hard work that Gordon, Dent and Batman attempted to do. Batman decided to take the fall for the Joker's deeds which caused the trio's legal work to be maintained, but Gotham City turned against Batman. Police with police dogs chased down Batman; however, Batman escaped and became a fugitive. This scene showed the importance of legally dealing with Batman's enemies and Batman becoming what Schatz (1981) called "the ultimate victim", which fits *The Dark Knight* into the genre of the evolved detective.

Two scenes; the Joker's assassination attempt on the mayor and the standoff between the Joker's men and the Gotham City Police will be analyzed as an example of the Joker's blending ability and the transferable aspect of the clown masks that the Joker and his men used. This paper will imply a connection between this and the work Black (2004) did in what he referred to as "Game-like elements."

Three final scenes; the Joker visiting Harvey Dent in the hospital, the Joker crashing the meeting of the mobs, and Batman catches the Joker will be briefly mentioned. The Joker with Dent will be referenced as an example of creating false control over the uncontrollable. The meetings of the mobs shall be used to further discuss the Joker as a terrorist. Batman and the Joker will be used as an example of terrorism vs. counterterrorism.

ASSUMPTIONS

This paper examined the artifacts: Batman/Bruce Wayne, the Joker, and the 2008 film *The Dark Knight*. These are fictitious artifacts based on elements of a comic book series from the 1930s. While this paper will compare these fictitious items to the real events of September 11, 2001, it is not the intent of this paper to make light of the real events of the 9/11 tragedy. The views established by this paper between the fictitious artifacts, the paradigms of rhetorical criticism's genre criticism, generic application, and semiotics are based on interpretations that may not have been the intent of its creators.

LIMITATIONS

This paper also makes no claims that the analysis is universally accepted outside Western culture particularly outside North America and regions of Europe. The views of this paper are not accepted by everyone as a way of viewing the world. Due to the sheer amount of source material available for the Batman universe, certain aspects might have been missed. The Batman universe contains stories and characters that have spanned generations and continues to expand with no end in sight. Cinematically *The Dark Knight* is constructed of various elements from the established Batman mythos and a fictitious film based on a comic book. Due to the composite nature of *The Dark Knight* it should be noted that many visual and sound elements were orchestrated in the hopes of achieving its greatest effect possible for each particular scene in order to provoke a certain thought, emotion or concept from its audience. This manufactured product was to explore concepts of Western American culture and may or may not be based on a real life individual. This echoes what was stated in Chapter Two about film noir. While *The Dark Knight* may seem realistic, it actually used "realist" conventions and techniques to present a convincing film. However, *The Dark Knight* remains a highly formal text.

CONCLUSION

This chapter attempted to make clear the methodology involved in analyzing the artifacts. The following chapter will apply the methodology and present the results found in *The Dark Knight*, attempting to provide examples that *The Dark Knight* may be a working modern myth with 9/11 and post-9/11 American cultural references. These references have been reinterpreted to better suit the Batman universe as seen in *The Dark Knight*. This chapter also implied identifiable film genre characteristics to better identify working semiotics in *The Dark Knight*.

CHAPTER 4
ANALYSIS OF THE DATA

THIS PAPER'S PREVIOUS CHAPTERS HAVE established prior research and the methodology that was used in the examination of the 2008 film *The Dark Knight*. This chapter will present the results. Chapter three mentioned certain scenes that will be analyzed. The criteria for scene selection include:

- Batman and/or the Joker need to be present or referred to in the scene.

- The action seen or concepts discussed need to reflect post-9/11 culture.

The Dark Knight was the second part of a three part series: *Batman Begins*, *The Dark Knight*, and *The Dark Knight Rises*. It was decided that this paper was to focus on *The Dark Knight* with minimal references to *Batman Begins*. *Batman Begins* was an origin story that established the universe of *The Dark Knight*. This allowed *The Dark Knight* the luxury of time to develop the plot. The Batman mythos was established by the various issues of the Batman comic book universe.

THE OPENING SEQUENCE AND FILM NOIR

The beginnings of many films and novels are very important because they ground the audience into the world they are about to enter. Beginnings also prep the audience for what to expect in the upcoming story. During the first twelve minutes of *The Dark Knight* the audience is welcomed by dark production company logos, very little sound and subtle music. A jarring cut presented a bright day with scattered buildings. A group of bank robbers hired by the Joker, attack a mob run bank. The robbers' clothes are common and nothing identifiable stands out except for the different rubber clown masks each robber wears. A trend was identified with the robbers; each time a member of the robbers completed their specialized work, they were killed by a nearby robber with the promise of the killer getting the victim's share of the loot. The Joker revealed himself at the end of the robbery as the sole surviving member of his gang and escaped in a school bus.

Following the bank robbery the audience is plunged into the darkness of a Gotham City night. The once bright day lit buildings are now silhouettes with occasional dotted office lights gleaming through the buildings' windows. Between these bleak monolithic monuments a weak beam of light shines through the night, the light is the Bat signal and it was activated by Gotham City Police Captain James Gordon. *Batman Begins* was the first part of the Nolan Batman series. *Batman Begins* established the Bat signal as a device Gordon could use to contact Batman. However, Gordon confessed to a fellow officer that Gordon did not need to speak with Batman. Tonight Gordon was reminding Gotham City that Batman was out there. Gordon was using the Bat signal as a crime deterrent, which did stop a drug deal.

Batman appeared in a parking garage to prevent a drug deal involving the Scarecrow, a villain from the previous film *Batman Begins*. Batman had difficulty dealing with criminals and a group of "Batman Copycats," but Batman was able to stop the criminals and arrest everyone. The Batman Copycats were a group of vigilantes who dressed up like Batman and attempted to stop crime. However, they did not have the advanced weapons and training that Batman did, which created more work for Batman.

All these moments helped the viewing audience become interested in *The Dark Knight* and follows what Vernet (1999) wrote about film noir beginnings being tranquil and identifying the characters. Through silent opening credits with the stillness of the Gotham City skyline, the silence was disrupted by the Joker's men following the Joker's plans to rob the bank. Audience members then understood the roles of the Joker as a villain, James Gordon as an ally to Batman and Batman as the hero. During this opening sequence another character was introduced and that was the character of Gotham City. As Schatz (1981) stated, the city represents society and its citizens. Gotham City and the citizens shall be what Batman and the Joker will fight over throughout *The Dark Knight*. With the silent opening credits, the establishment of characters; the Joker, Gordon, Batman and the city, we are able to identify *The Dark Knight* as a film with the stylistic flair of film noir.

THE ATTACKS OF SEPTEMBER 11, 2001

The opening sequence established the location as Gotham City with criminal activity occurring during the day. During the bank robbery we identified the Joker as a villain who secretly made a deal with the criminals he hired. Through ruthless cunning, the Joker eliminates the other gang members, becomes the sole robbery survivor, and escapes the heist. Through these opening scenes, the Joker robbed a mob owned bank and was responsible for killing his own men. Alleged terrorists have been accused of being responsible for killing their own men to further their own cause. On September 11, 2001 small terrorist groups took control of airplanes with the goal of crashing them into planned targets. One of the terrorist targets was the World Trade Center buildings. The attacks happened in broad daylight and the targets were financial buildings. After the attacks, Osama bin Laden, leader of the terrorist group Al-Qaeda claimed responsibility for the attacks. These events were the start of America's War on Terror. The opening sequence of *The Dark Knight* involved a financial institution that was attacked during the day by the Joker who claimed responsibility for the crime to the police and the mobs via the banks surveillance cameras. As Jung (2010) pointed out, post-9/11 films are a spectacle of real life images with narratives mixed with terrorist violence.

THE JOKER'S BANK ROBBERY

During this scene the audience was introduced to the Joker and given a glimpse into how he operates. At first it was unknown to the audience and the robbers that the Joker was among them due to the rubber clown masks all the robbers wore. It did not seem that the robbers knew each other and there did not seem to be a clear leader. While the robbers were working for the Joker it was implied through the robbers' dialogue that they have never met the Joker. The bank was robbed and as each of the Joker's men completes their task, they were quickly killed by another member of the group in the promise that the killer would get the victim's share of the loot. Eventually the only person left was the Joker, who took all the money from the bank robbery. The Joker escaped in a school bus, which merged with a convoy of other identical buses.

Jones (2008) wrote about "leaderless groups" (p. 7). In the bank robbery scene we learn the Joker recruited his men secretly. While they were working for the Joker, the Joker just gave the robbers instructions and they followed them. When the bank robbery occurred there was no clear physical leader. The robbers were following the orders of someone they never met in person. This "leaderless group" is similar to how terrorists recruit people for their causes. The recruits were instructed what to do, then how to meet up with others; becoming a group in order to accomplish their task.

TERRORIST BLENDING

The Joker was able to successfully blend into his environment twice during the bank robbery scene; once when he was dressed in shabby clothes with a rubber clown mask. This was similar to the appearance of his fellow bank robbers. The second was while he shifted a dusty school bus into gear, merging with a line of identical school buses and escaping the bank robbery.

Through these examples the Joker can blend in among his criminal cohorts and the public. The Joker's ability to blend continued throughout *The Dark Knight*. During the assassination attempt on the Mayor, the Joker successfully disguised himself as part of the honor guard. Also Batman had great difficulty finding the Joker as he hid in Gotham City. As Black (2004) stated, "terrorism operates on small scale hit-and-run tactics… [and] camouflage themselves as ordinary civilians in urban [settings]" (p. 17). Schatz (1981) also referred to the city as a representation of the citizens who occupy it. This may be interpreted as the Joker was always hiding among the mass of citizens.

GAME-LIKE ELEMENTS

The Joker's men did not have a clear uniform. The only physically identifiable thing they wore was a rubber clown mask. An interesting aspect of the clown masks that the Joker's men used, was that they were removable, meaning they cannot be trusted as a true identifier of the wearer being part of the Joker's gang. Symbolically anyone could wear the rubber clown masks. This was proven twice in *The Dark Knight*. The first time was during the Joker's assassination attempt on the mayor because the Joker and his men did not wear their identifiable clown masks. The second time was at the end of *The Dark Knight* during the police standoff: the Joker's men put their clown masks on the medical hostages. This tactic fooled the police into believing the disguised medical hostages were the Joker's men. The transferable quality of the rubber clown masks implied that anyone could potentially be a member of the Joker's group. An implication might be made that the Joker is Osama Bin Laden in a post-9/11 world and his men are terrorists. Symbolically the rubber clown masks implied that anyone might potentially be a terrorist. Black (2004) commented earlier about terrorism having a "lack of game-like elements" (p. 16). The true identity of terrorists was an issue in real life with Allied troops during the conflict in the Middle East due to the terrorists not having clear game-like elements like uniforms and being able to blend in an urban setting as civilians which was similar to the Joker and his men.

TERRORIST: THE MODERN OTHER

Rodriguez (2010) and Camp et al. (2010) identified a number of psychological problems that the Joker had. Tuman (2010) introduced the aspect of "The Other" while Jung (2010) explained the concept further by stating that some "terrorist others" are homegrown with mental disorders. Kolenic (2009) also observed that *The Dark Knight* Joker was either psychotic or the only sane person in Gotham. However, Batman as a general character and *The Dark Knight* Batman also fit Jung's (2010) definition of a "terrorist other". Even though Batman had experienced the world, Batman is still a homegrown terrorist who has his own psychological issues that stem from witnessing the murder of his parents as a child.

THE BAT SIGNAL

Following the Joker's bank robbery is a montage; it is night and the Gotham

City skyline is dotted with lights and darkened silhouettes of buildings. Through the clustered monolithic buildings, a spotlight flickers to life, the light pierced the night. The spotlight is the "Bat signal" which causes a police officer to smile and a drug dealer to cancel his transaction with a pleading customer.

A conversation was heard, it is an interview with the mayor. The topic is how Gotham City was struggling with crime, but the vigilante known as Batman has started to aid in the cleanup of Gotham. Batman is a vigilante and it was discovered that official policy was to arrest Batman. The source of the Bat signal is a modified spotlight on the rooftop of the Gotham City Police Department where police captain James Gordon waits. A fellow officer joins Gordon with a hot drink for Gordon. Their conversation implied that the signal is used to contact Batman. Gordon has worked with Batman in *Batman Begins*, but tonight Gordon does not need to talk with Batman. Instead, Gordon was reminding Gotham that Batman is out there.

Police Captain James Gordon used the Bat signal as a deterrent for criminal activity. This may be compared to how an empty police car with its lights on, reduces speeding cars due to the fact that the passing motorists believe there might be a police officer in the squad car. Gordon's tactics proved to be successful when a drug deal was cancelled once the dealer noticed the Bat signal in the sky. The character of James Gordon gives the impression of a law officer who might take necessary risks to maintain order in Gotham City. Gordon is breaking the law because officially the police are supposed to arrest the vigilante known as Batman.

THE COLOR-CODE SYSTEM

In the months following the attacks of 9/11 a visual system was used as a way to provide structure during a time of chaos. This system was known as the color-code system. If intelligence was gathered that a possible terrorist attack was imminent, a color would signal the likelihood of there being a terrorist attack. The color-code system could fluctuate on a daily basis. However, both the Bat signal and color-code system suffered from an issue of vagueness, mixed messages and potential unmonitored manipulation. The Bat signal may have a clear message between Gordon and Batman; but it also sent the mixed message to the citizens of Gotham that Batman was needed even though he was not.

The possible abuse of both devices was what Paul and Park (2009) pointed out earlier in regard to the possible abuse of the Color-Coded System. There was never any guaranteed system or safeguards to prevent the unwarranted manipulation of both devices. The Bat signal was also an indicator that Gotham City was reliant on a vigilante, instead of the established government. Throughout *The Dark Knight* one of the Joker's messages was that structure was an illusion. The Joker visited Harvey Dent in the hospital and explained that if a bunch of soldiers died, it was expected because it was "part of the plan." However, if the Joker made a threat on one mayor, everyone in Gotham City went crazy because the Joker's action was not part of the plan. It may be interpreted that the Joker's message is that establishing a type of structure over the uncontrollable, gives people the false illusion of control and order. Gordon's use of the Bat signal may be seen as an attempt to give the citizens of Gotham City the sense of false control and order. Much like the Color-Coded System was implying a type of control and order in case of further terrorist attacks on American soil.

BATMAN AS A TERRORIST

Black (2004) mentioned that terrorists are motivated by a, "restoration of the past" (p.18). In *The Dark Knight* when the Joker crashed the Gotham mob boss meeting, he revealed that he wanted to turn the clock back to a time in Gotham before Batman. However, the Joker's reliability is questionable. The Joker might be saying this just to manipulate the mob bosses. Someone who was motivated by a "restoration of the past" was Batman. *Batman Begins* and *The Dark Knight* Batman was motivated to restore Gotham City to its once splendid glory. The city with less crime is the Gotham that Bruce Wayne remembered as a child. *Batman Begins* had Ra's al Ghoul who trained Wayne in order to have him return to Gotham and lead it to its destruction because Gotham has become too crime ridden and corrupt. Wayne refused and believed that Gotham City could still be saved.

Jung's (2010) vigilante myth was based on an individual who was wronged and society offered no answers. In *Batman Begins*, when Bruce Wayne (Batman) was a child he lost his parents when they were killed. Their murderer was later assassinated by a local mob boss. Wayne developed the identity of Batman, a vigilante who aids in the arrest of criminals through illegal means. While it can be implied that Batman fits with Jung's definition of the vigilante myth. Black (2004) said that "terrorism is a particularly aggressive form of justice" (p. 22). While Batman may be a vigilante, his actions of restoring the past imply that he could be a terrorist.

THE BATMAN COPYCATS

Bruce Wayne forged a secret identity in Christopher Nolan's *Batman Begins*, which carried over into *The Dark Knight*. Wayne through Batman lived by an established set of morals and led by example. As Zehnder and Calvert (2003) stated earlier, the hero teaches us what we should aspire to. Batman's leading example was absorbed by the citizens in a city over run with crime. Groups of vigilante citizens referred to as "copycats", formed wanting to help Batman. It may be seen as the citizens were converted to Batman's philosophy of literally fighting crime.

Zinnbauer and Pargament (1998) wrote that converted individuals are usually seeking something to resolve their difficulties. Batman's dedication to a greater cause of improving Gotham City inspired and converted Gotham City civilians into the Batman Copycats. The Batman Copycats were physically changing themselves by dressing like Batman and putting themselves in the path of danger by attempting to stop crime against Batman's wishes. Batman was against the Batman Copycats helping him because they did not have the proper technology, funding and training that Batman had. Batman remarked to Alfred his disapproval of the Batman Copycats in *The Dark Knight* by saying, "That wasn't exactly what I had in mind when I said I wanted to inspire people."

To the Batman Copycats, Batman was what Jones (2008) meant as the "something greater than their own ego" (p. 5), which gave them a sense of purpose and values. Desai (2004) said that vigilantism can quickly expand into larger groups that question established order. This was evident with the formation of the Batman Copycats. To a degree, *The Dark Knight* Joker might be seen as a hybrid Batman Copycat. In *Batman Begins* and *The Dark Knight,* Batman helped police to legally arrest corrupt authority figures. In *The Dark Knight* instead of helping to arresting corrupt authority figures the Joker killed any authority figure. The Joker could be a product of Batman's misinterpreted vigilantism message due to Desai's (2004) contention about the spread of vigilantism. Similar to Jung's (2004) vigilante myth about movements questioning social order, the actions of Batman, the Batman Copycats and the Joker may be seen as each questioning established social order in different ways.

THE JOKER'S VIDEOTAPE

In *The Dark Knight* a news broadcast began that talked about the Joker killing someone dressed as Batman. The broadcast displayed the hanged dead body of a Batman Copycat, dressed as Batman but his face was mutilated to look like the Joker. The body was lowered from a building from which the Joker or one of his men had strung it. The broadcast then played a crudely made video created by the Joker involving the Batman Copycat victim. In the video the Joker mocked and tormented the Batman Copycat. The Joker then turned the camera on himself and said, "You see this is how crazy Batman has made Gotham." The Joker's message in the recording was that Batman was the real problem for the city because Batman was the cause of the Batman Copycats. The Joker was trying to appeal to the citizens of Gotham. The Joker's actions might be seen as an attempt to show the citizens of Gotham how institutions and order are just illusions. This point was also mentioned when the Joker was visiting Harvey Dent in the hospital. While the Joker's message can be implied as delusional and paranoid, Kolenic (2009) pointed out that the Joker's actions may also be interpreted as someone who speaks the truth.

Following the attacks of 9/11, America's new enemies were terrorists who incorporated different tactics in order to dishearten and withdraw American soldiers from the war. The terrorists started video recording the beheading of Americans and posting the uncensored videos online. This public mutilation was effective in decreasing the moral of American troops and was successful in America's previous conflicts. Included in the beheading videos were messages from the terrorists. The messages would explain why the terrorists were executing the victim and that the terrorists would continue fighting till America withdrew its troops. As Costigan (2007) wrote, public mutilation was a way to dishearten people in order to force public policy. As pointed out in Chapter Two: Osama bin Laden made a videotape which stated the terrorists were not to blame and in the upcoming election between Kerry and Bush, the American people's future was in their own hands. A parallel might be interpreted that the Joker was similar to Osama bin Laden. Both videotape messages were an attempt to convince the American people and citizens of Gotham City that they were the ones who really held the true power.

BATMAN'S SONAR TECHNOLOGY

In Chapter Two Ip (2012) established a connection between *The Dark Knight* and the increase of US surveillance on its own people in the days following the attacks of 9/11. This section shall attempt to add to those observations. *The Dark Knight* Batman needed to find the Joker. But as established earlier in this chapter, the Joker was very difficult to locate due to his ability to blend in. Batman had to resort to illegal surveillance through the advanced wiretapping of mobile phones in order to find the Joker. While the wiretapping was on, Batman was able to locate the Joker anytime he used a mobile phone. The drawback was that Batman was spying on millions of innocent Gotham City citizens without the citizens knowing. The citizens also did not give Batman their consent.

While many of Batman's activities and violent nature may be classified as illegal but quickly shrugged off, the wiretapping incident was highlighted in *The Dark Knight* when Lucius Fox stated, "Spying on 30 million people isn't part of my job description." Understanding the urgency of finding the Joker, Fox reluctantly agreed to aid Batman and they were able to find the Joker. Following the attacks of 9/11 America established the "P.A.T.R.I.O.T. Act" with the hopes of increasing national security. As mentioned by Scheppele (2004), included in the PATRIOT Act was the increased use of electronic surveillance. Simone (2009) said that innocent Americans could be part of "a roving surveillance without their knowledge or expressed consent" (p. 3). A connection may be drawn to Batman's wiretap sonar and the American government's wiretap spying. Both were also justified as a tool to potentially locate terrorists.

TERRORISM VS. COUNTERTERRORISM

A further example of terrorism versus counterterrorism can be seen at the end of *The Dark Knight*. When the Joker was saved by Batman, Batman told the Joker, "You'll be in a padded cell, forever." This implied that Batman believed the Joker could be cured and eventually understood. Batman's vision of the Joker's future was anything but the Joker being killed. However, as Rodriguez (2010) stated, "The Joker, like madness itself, cannot be annihilated but he can be isolated, diagnosed and compelled to enter a therapeutic discourse" (p. 17). While Batman will not kill the Joker, the Joker will not kill Batman because the Joker sees Batman as being "too much fun."

The cat and mouse game between them is destined to continue with no foreseeable end in sight. As the Joker said, "I think you and I are destined to do this forever." Black (2004) stated, "Once begun, terrorism and counterterrorism may exhibit feud-like elements of vengeance, each side answering aggression with aggression, a process that may extend over many years" (p. 18). The Joker seems like a terrorist while Batman who responds to the Joker's activity is a counterterrorist. Black (2004) connected terrorism with other social control. During *The Dark Knight* the Joker performed two types of experiments: "The Ticking Bomb Scenario" and "The Prisoner's Dilemma." The Ticking Bomb Scenario is a debate of morality and rights, while The Prisoner's Dilemma is an exercise in game theory. Both of these scenarios may be classified as impacting society and imply a type of social control. Nelson (2008) pointed out that superheroes may act against social control, and Black (2004) mentioned that terrorism was a type of social control and "justice in response to crime that is itself a form of justice" (p. 22). The Nolan Batman may seem like a terrorist and vigilante. However, his actions are in response to the death of his parents; while the Joker wreaks havoc in the streets of Gotham, with killing sprees and kidnappings in an attempt to open the eyes of the citizens of Gotham City to the chaos that Batman has caused. Batman's actions are that of preventing the Joker from doing further damage. Combined with Black's (2004) statement, the Joker's activity and attempts to manipulate societal change may imply that the Joker is a terrorist. Batman's actions imply that he may also be a terrorist. However, Batman's actions are a response for justice, according to Black's definitions, this might label Batman as a counterterrorist.

BATMAN INTERROGATES THE JOKER

In *The Dark Knight* the Joker is caught but District Attorney Harvey Dent was reported missing. The newly appointed Police Commissioner James Gordon decided to talk to the Joker. Gordon entered a dimly lit interrogation cell where the Joker waited handcuffed sitting behind a metallic table. Gordon realized questioning was not going anywhere and decided to let Batman interrogate the Joker. The Joker revealed that he kidnapped Dent and Rachel Dawes. The Joker limited information about himself, leaving the police and Batman to have nothing to threaten him with. The only leverage Batman had on the Joker was the use of physical torture. Batman proceeded to beat the Joker, but it proved ineffective. Finally the Joker gave them misinformation as part of his overall plan.

Allhoff (2003) previously stated that America used indirect methods in order to torture terrorist suspects without any direct American involvement. Usually suspects were tortured by non-Americans while American agents who were in the same room, recorded the terrorists' confessions. In *The Dark Knight* when the Joker was in police custody James Gordon allowed Batman to physically beat the Joker in the hopes of locating Harvey Dent and Rachel Dawes. In this situation, a parallel may be drawn with the police representing American agents, while Batman was the third party who illegally tortured the terrorist. However, the game that the Joker played on the police and Batman might be interpreted as a variation of "The Ticking Bomb Scenario."

THE TICKING BOMB SCENARIO

The following is a summary of what was stated in Chapter Two about the Ticking Bomb scenario: A suspect was captured by police. It is discovered that the suspect had hidden a bomb that was going to explode but the location of the bomb and when the bomb was going to explode is unknown.

The suspect refuses to cooperate with law officials, leading to the debate of the scenario. Some of the questions are should torture be used on the suspect to discover the location of the bomb? Do the suspect's rights outweigh the rights of the bomb's potential victims? If torture is used on the suspect, then should officials respond to the bomb's location, possibly risking more lives? Is the information gained through torture accurate? When the scenario was applied to *The Dark Knight*, it might be seen that the Joker was the potential bomber. However, the Joker gave misinformation.

MISINFORMATION

Mayerfeld (2008) insisted that when faced with the "Ticking Bomb Scenario," time is critical so torture is justified. The prevention of innocent lives becoming victims is a good reason to resort to that savage act of interrogation. This was an issue that people in a post-9/11 world faced; was torture acceptable? If so what type of torture was allowed? Shane and Savage (2011) pointed out that torture allowed US troops to locate Osama bin Laden.

Ip (2012) stated that *The Dark Knight's* Batman was never successful in gaining information through torture. Prior to the Joker's interrogation, Batman threw a mob boss off the side of a building in an attempt to get information on the Joker's location. The mobster did not know the Joker's location and Batman's attempt to gain information failed. In the interrogation scene, Batman's application of torture once again failed. While Batman's torture might not have been successful in *The Dark Knight*, torture could be seen as an expected tool for Batman to utilize. Batman's past qualified him as a vigilante mythic hero which Jung (2010) stated be allowed to use excessive force. Black (2004) also pointed out that the war against terrorists is an unconventional war and counterterrorism would likely include torture as a tool to gain intelligence.

THE JOKER'S "PRISONER'S DILEMMA"

This section shall attempt to extend the connections Ip (2012) created between this scene, "The Prisoner's Dilemma" and a post-9/11 by focusing on the importance of the role cooperation has in this scenario. In *The*

Dark Knight, the Joker performed a variation of a social experiment known as "The Prisoner's Dilemma." The Prisoner's Dilemma is an exercise in game theory. The following is a brief summary from what was explained in Chapter Two. Two individuals are captured. The captors separate the individuals and attempt to compel the individuals to betray the trust of the other. This is accomplished by the captors enticing the individuals by offering a reduced sentence. The captors are relying on the selfishness of the individuals to betray each other. The solution of the dilemma is mutual cooperation on behalf of the individuals. To an extent the dilemma was seen in the Joker's bank robbery scene. The Joker's men killed each other off one at a time for the selfish goal of getting a larger share of the loot, not taking into consideration that the Joker made the same deal with all of his men. But the Joker performed the dilemma to a greater extent at the end of *The Dark Knight*.

Two evacuation ferries were filled with Gotham citizens on one and Gotham criminals on the other. The Joker cuts power to both ferries and informs the ships that they are filled with explosives and the detonator of their respective ferry is located on the other boat. The Joker demanded that one of the boats blow up the other, if one boat was not detonated by midnight, the Joker would blow up both vessels. The citizens took a vote, the vote went in favor of blowing up the inmates, but none of the passengers could physically activate the detonator. On the inmates' ferry, one of the inmates asked for the detonator and tossed it overboard. At midnight, both boats remained floating to the Joker's disappointment. It is implied that the Joker played the role of the captor. The two boats were the imprisoned individuals. The reward was their lives. However, unlike the bank robbery, the Joker's boat hostages were firm in cooperation. The notion of humans favoring cooperation concurs with the statement from, studies conducted by "Can We Eliminate Evil?" (2012). "Can We Eliminate Evil?" believed that humans have evolved to understand the benefits of mutual cooperation, as opposed to selfish individualism.

The Gotham citizens and prisoners sent a message to The Joker with his variation of the Prisoner's Dilemma. By not blowing each other up, the captives' choice was in favor of mutual cooperation which Reboul (2006) stated was the correct choice for the dilemma, "The moral from the

Prisoner's Dilemma is that initiating cooperation is important and it has to be admitted" (p. 480). After the attacks of 9/11, the majority of Americans came together in unity, maintaining a level of social control, though they were in fear of what further terrorist attacks were to come.

FILM NOIR AND FEAR

In Chapter Two, Jung (2012) said that paranoia and fear were being expressed in post-9/11 film. *Batman Begins* and *The Dark Knight* relied on the application of fear. Batman used "Gothic Fear" against his criminal enemies; in *Batman Begins* Bruce Wayne started to form a secret identity. Wayne chose the symbol of a bat and became Batman. When his butler, Alfred asked why, Wayne replied, "Bats frighten me. It's time my enemies shared my dread." According to Kolenic (2009), *The Dark Knight* Joker used terroristic fear on the citizens of Gotham in an attempt to expose Gotham's flawed government system. James Gordon attempted to establish a system utilizing the Bat signal in order to gain false control over the unknown fear. The Joker tried to prove his points by using variations of the "Ticking Bomb Scenario," and the "Prisoner's Dilemma." Schlesinger (2010) said that *The Dark Knight's* Joker was "a terrorist whose motives and methods defy understanding and predictability" (p. 138). Schlesinger (2010) also commented on the parallels between the film, its marketing campaign and 9/11. Russell (1998) suggested that a horror film's monster "stands in for social disorder and rampant desire" (p. 237). These various plot points imply a stronger connection with how fear was being used in the Nolan films and a post-9/11 world.

THE GANGSTER GENRE

Farber (1999) described the gangster as someone who had rugged individualist characteristics, but stripped away moral rationalizations. During the bank robbery scene, the Joker tricked his thugs into killing each other, leaving him the lone survivor with all the money. In this scene the Joker robbed from a mob controlled bank, The Joker was responsible for the death of the bank robbers and killed the getaway driver. While these actions may insinuate that the Joker is a vigilante with extremely violent methods, the Joker was exercising his individualism. Throughout

The Dark Knight as Kolenic (2009) stated, the Joker was trying to show the citizens of Gotham City that structure and institutions of control were all an illusion. To the Joker anarchy was the true answer. The Joker only targeted authority figures; however, at the end of the film with the Joker's "Prisoner's Dilemma" the Joker targeted citizens in an attempt to get them directly involved. In one of the Joker's video messages, the Joker asked the citizens; what will it take to get you involved? Schatz (1981) pointed out that the failure of the gangster comes from the conflict between individual success and the common good. The Joker realized his defeat at the end of *The Dark Knight* when the boats of citizens and criminals did not blow each other up. In this moment the representative strength of Gotham City stood up against the Joker and proved to be more powerful than the Joker expected.

THE EVOLVED DETECTIVE GENRE

Schatz (1981) stated that one of the most common genres is the Western. The Western genre contained modern American myths and the hero represents both order and savagery. This goes along with Jung's (2010) statement that a Western is conflicting values. Ip (2012) added that Westerns are rooted in pop culture. Schatz (1981) stated that the Western hero evolved into the detective, where the hero fought for a utopian community. Farber (1999) pointed out that violence is celebrated in this genre. From there Schatz's (1981) hero evolved into the evolved detective with the critical aspect that the hero was at risk and could be the ultimate victim. *The Dark Knight* Batman struggled to restore the Gotham City that he remembers as a youth. His appearance, use of gothic fear and unbalanced psychological background as explained by Zehnder and Calvert (2003), allude to the fact that Batman may be more villain than hero. Batman's delicate balancing act of not becoming a villain keeps us interested in the character of Batman. Due to his weaknesses Batman is seen as more human. While the Joker did his best to disrupt Batman, at the end of *The Dark Knight* Batman sacrificed his name and reputation so that the Joker would not win. This caused Batman to become *The Dark Knight*'s ultimate victim. The effect of Batman's action caused the Gotham City that he protected to turn against him. The act of Batman becoming an outcast falls in line with Schatz's

(1981) "Vengeful hero" who because of his isolation and static psychological being, "finally enforce social order but necessitate his departure from the community he has saved" (p. 57). *The Dark Knight* concluded with the city turning its back on Batman.

THE LAST LAUGH

Farber (1999) said that, "every attempt to succeed is an act of aggression, leaving one alone and guilty and defenseless among enemies: one is *punished* for success" (p. 48). *The Dark Knight* ends with the three characters that we were introduced to in the first twelve minutes as failures because of their attempts to succeed. The Joker is captured and the city proved him wrong in his assumptions about society. James Gordon stands among the masses, bearing the guilt of a lie in order to protect the city. This dirty, hidden truth is what Schatz (1981) stated was part of the evolved detective genre. Batman retreats from the angry city that he sacrificed almost everything for. *The Dark Knight* reflected these issues and did not give a solution to the viewers of how they should live in a post-9/11 world. Since *The Dark Knight* reflected a post-9/11 world, it not only qualified as a modern myth but the use of referential images and narrative fulfilled Jung's (2010) earlier definition of an aspect of a post-9/11 film.

CONCLUSION

This chapter presented the findings of all the previous chapters and attempted to strengthen connections between *The Dark Knight* and a post-9/11 world. The next chapter will be the concluding chapter with recommendations and final thoughts on the subject.

CHAPTER 5
CONCLUSION

THROUGH THE GENERATIONS THE BATMAN character has been reinvented in order to reflect modern times. Initially starting off as a comic book, Batman adapted to the big screen and was invited into homes via color televisions. Batman holds connections with mythology. With his constant struggle to resist the temptations of a criminal lifestyle, and do what is right, Batman's example can be seen as a working modern myth that we may look to as a source of philosophical guidance and a distraction from the troubles of life.

Batman began in 1939 as a comic book hero who stopped criminals. The 1943 *Batman* serial was released during the time of World War II when America was fighting Germany and Japan. Batman was working for the government and his foe was Japanese scientist Dr. Daka. America's war against Japan might be the cause of the creation of an entirely new villain for Batman. The sequel *Batman & Robin* was released in 1949, four years after 1945 which was the end of World War II. In this installment Batman had his sidekick Robin and no Dr. Daka.

The Adam West Batman was next in 1968. This interpretation was a television show that utilized color television with colorful props and costumes. Instead of being serious, Batman and his alter ego Bruce Wayne were hipsters who exhibited knowledge and respect of the Eastern world. Technically, the Adam West Batman was the first to have a live action Batman in color on television and in movie theaters.

The Tim Burton and Joel Schumacher versions returned Batman to the big screen. With the aid of the stylistic film noir, Tim Burton's 1989 *Batman* set the stage for being a darker, serious Batman. During the 90s interest in the family was seen in the form of family comedies and the unknown lurked with the upcoming millennium. Burton's Batman was a stark opposite from the loud, brightly colored Adam West Batman. However, as the interest in animated cartoons began populating television programming, Joel Schumacher's Batman slowly returned to the comedic tones originally seen in the Adam West Batman.

Christopher Nolan's *Batman Begins* and *The Dark Knight* reflected a culture recovering from the tragedy of September 11, 2001. The Nolan Batman in *Batman Begins* was accepted into a terrorist cult who hid in the mountains and zealously believed in upholding justice and order at any cost. Batman decided to take a stand against them as they organized to strike the densely populated metropolitan Gotham City. The parallel might be drawn to America's post-9/11 enemy, hiding behind extreme religious beliefs as they plot in their unknown mountain retreats, sending terror cells to attack specific urban targets.

Batman was going to war against a cult and his Batmobile reflected that. Batman's personal vehicle known as the Batmobile was an extension of Batman's character. Previous versions of the Batmobile were ornately decorated with fins that resembled bat wings and a couple had glowing neon giving the Batmobile an otherworldly organic aura. However, Nolan's Batman was the first to have a military-esc Batmobile that had a stout tank-like appearance. It was also never referred to as "The Batmobile" in *Batman Begins*, it was instead referred to as "The Tumbler." *The Dark Knight* would be when it would be referred to as the Batmobile.

Reflecting the current trend of television's police procedural dramas, Nolan's Batman relied on James Gordon which gave the Nolan Batman a more legal feel with his actions opposed to the previous Batman's "Devil-May-Care" attitude. One might be so bold as to suggest that if you were to remove Batman, the Joker and all comic book aspects from *The Dark Knight* and replace them with a private investigator and terrorist in a real world setting, most of the original story would remain intact as a cops and robbers drama. *The Dark Knight* not only concentrated the established philosophies of Batman and his enemy, but made things personal instead of religious and physically gave them the forms of Batman and the Joker where they actively did battle.

Both films displayed the harsh landscape of a post-9/11 world that was made stylistically starker through the use of film noir. While Burton's Batman was the first to use film noir, Nolan's Batman contained another level of film noir which employed the use of filters, and IMAX cameras to provide a gritty edge of realism to the characters of Gotham City. Characters that utilized fear and exaggerated villains that included a disturbed, face paint smudged Joker who seemed more monster than man. Sadly, Burton's questionable vision of a mutant-like Penguin in *Batman Returns*, did not successfully translate. While there have been connections drawn between *The Dark Knight's* Batman and President George W. Bush and *The Dark Knight's* Joker and Osama bin Laden, the debate continues on whether these comparisons are accurate and who was in the right. History shall provide the real answer for this since upon the initial release of *The Dark Knight* the Bush policies were seen as flawed, but they are now seen as a necessary evil for the time.

While myths reflect their host culture, myths have been used as a way to provide an explanation of how things operate. Working myths reflect their host culture and remain relevant by providing guidance to the audience on life events they have or may yet encounter. Batman the character has changed with the times and will continue to change in an effort to remain relevant. This paper explained how *The Dark Knight* displayed similarities with post-9/11 culture. These similarities were not present pre-9/11 society.

This paper also examined how the attacks of 9/11 triggered a chain reaction that changed the world. These events were so unbelievable that everything seemed to be the latest plot of a film or comic book instead of real life. As Morrison (2011) wrote,

> Traumatized by war footage and disaster clips, spied upon by ubiquitous surveillance cams, threatened by exotic villains who plot from their caverns and subterranean lairs, preyed upon by dark and monumental Gods of Fear, we are being

sucked inexorably into Comic Book Reality, with only moments to save the world, as usual. (p. xvii)

Therefore, *The Dark Knight* should be considered a working modern myth, and a good representation of post-9/11 cinema.

RECOMMENDATIONS

Recommendations for further study on the subject of modern myths and post-9/11 cinema from a film aspect would be *The Dark Knight Rises*, *V for Vendetta*, and *Iron Man*. These films were created during a post-9/11 world and might have post-9/11 film characteristics. These films are also adaptations from comic books. *The Dark Knight Rises* is the conclusion of the Nolan Batman series. *V for Vendetta* makes heavy use of fear and social conditioning. *Iron Man* was considered a success that changed how people view comic book films.

FUTURE STUDIES

Possible future studies might include:

– What roles have psychopathic characters developed into throughout the history of cinema?

– Is Christopher Nolan's final Batman film *The Dark Knight Rises* a post-9/11 modern working myth?

– Is post-9/11 cinema still relevant in current times or has another type of film replaced it?

REFERENCES

Allhoff, F. (2003). Terrorism and torture. *International Journal of Applied Philosophy. 17*(1) *105-118.* Retrieved from http://files.allhoff.org/research/Terrorism_and_Torture.pdf

Ashmore T. M. (1987, Winter). The prisoner's dilemma: A computer adaptation. *The Western Journal of Speech Communication. 51,117-126.* Retrieved from http://www.tandfonline.com/doi/abs/10.1080/10570318709374256#preview

Batman & Robin. (2014, January17). *Box office Mojo.* Retrieved from http://www.boxofficemojo.com/movies/?id=batmanrobin.htm

Batman & Robin. *Internet Movie Database.* (2014, January17). Retrieved from http://www.imdb.com/title/tt0118688/

Bilandzic, H., Sukalla, F., Herrmann, F., & Kinnebrock, S. (2008). What's the point of this film? What's the point of this genre? Analyzing moral messages of genre films. *Paper presented at the annual meeting of the International Communication Association, TBA, Montreal, Quebec, Canada*, May 21, 2008 [Abstract]. Retrieved from http://www.allacademic.com/meta/p233990_index.html

Black, D. (2004, March). The geometry of terrorism. *Sociological Theory, 22*(1), 14-25. *Theories of Terrorism: A Symposium.* doi: 10.2307/3648956

Bloodsworth-Lugo, M., & Lugo-Lugo, C. (2011, November 2). 9/11 goes to the movies: The ideological reverberations of "the day that changed America Forever." *Reconstruction: Studies in Contemporary Culture*. Retrieved from http://www.academia.edu/5471022/9_11_Goes_to_the_Movies_The_Ideological_Reverberations_of_The_Day_that_Changed_America_Forever_

Box Office Mojo. (1997). *Batman & Robin* [Motion Picture]. Retrieved from http://www.boxofficemojo.com/movies/?id=batmanrobin.htm

Box Office Mojo. (2008). *The Dark Knight* [Motion Picture]. Retrieved from http://www.boxofficemojo.com/movies/?id=darkknight.htm

Camp, M.E., Webster, C.R., Coverdale, T.R., Coverdale, J.H., & Nairn, R. (2010). The joker: A dark night for depictions of mental illness. *Academic Psychiatry, 34*(2), *145-149*. doi: 10.1176/appi.ap.34.2.145

Campbell, J. (1968). *The hero with a thousand faces.* Princeton, NJ: Princeton University Press.

"Can We Eliminate Evil?" (2012, July 18). *Through the Wormhole.* Science Channel. http://www.sciencechannel.com/tv-shows/through-the-wormhole/videos/eliminate-evil.htm

Chandler, D. (1994) *Semiotics for beginners.* Retrieved from http://users.aber.ac.uk/dgc/Documents/S4B/sem0a.html

Chojnacki, M.(2004, May 27). Cultural differences in game theory: Proposed variability of the individualist and collectivist in prisoner's dilemma [Abstract]. *Paper presented at the annual meeting of the International Communication Association, New Orleans Sheraton, New Orleans, LA.* Retrieved http://www.allacademic.com/meta/p112738_index.html

Cobley, P., Jansz, L. (1997). *Introducing semiotics.* New York, NY: Totem Books.

Costigan, S. (2007). Terrorists and the internet: Crashing or cashing in? [Abstract]. *Terrornomics*, 1-27. Retrieved from http://papers.ssrn.com/sol3/papers.cfm?abstract_id=1634299

Desai, A. (2004). The cape of good dope? A post-apartheid story of gangs and vigilantes [Abstract]. *Globalization, Marginalization & New Social Movements in post-Apartheid South Africa, University of Kwazulu-Natal*, 1-33. Retrieved from http://ccs.ukzn.ac.za/files/Desai%20Pagad%20Research%20Report.pdf

Dittmer, J. (2005). Captain America's empire: Reflections of identity, popular culture, and post-9/11 geopolitics [Abstract]. *Annals of the Association of American Geographers, 95*(3), 626-643. Retrieved from http://www.jstor.org/stable/3693960?origin=JSTOR-pdf

Dixon, W. W. (2003). *Visions of the apocalypse: Spectacles of destruction in American cinema*. New York, NY: Wallflower Press.

Dozier, W. (Producer), Martianson, L. (Director). (1966). *Batman: The Movie* [Motion Picture]. USA: 20th Century Fox.

Ebert, R. (2008, July 16). The dark knight. *Chicago Sun-Times*. Retrieved from http://rogerebert.suntimes.com/apps/pbcs.dll/article?AID=/20080716/reviews/55996637

Ewing, D., Jr. (1999). Film noir: Style and content. *Film Noir Reader 2*, 73-83. New York, NY: Limelight Editions.

Farber, S. (1999). Violence and the bitch goddess. *Film Noir Reader 2*, 45-55. New York, NY: Limelight Editions.

Fisher, M. (2006). Gothic oedipus: Subjectivity and capitalism in Christopher Nolan's Batman Begins [Abstract]. *Imagetext: Interdisciplinary Comic Studies, 2*(2). Retrieved from http://www.english.ufl.edu/imagetext/archives/v2_2/fisher/index.shtml

Flowthow, R.C. (Producer), Hillyer, L. (Director). (1943). *Batman* [Film Serial]. USA: Columbia Pictures.

Foss, S.K. (2004). *Retorical criticism*. Long Grove, IL: Waveland Press.

FoxNews.com. (2004, October 30). *Bin Laden claims responsibility for 9/11.* Retrieved from http://www.foxnews.com/story/0,2933,137095,00.html

Guber, P., Peters, J., Melniker B., & Uslan, M. (Producers), Burton, T. (Director). (1989). *Batman* [Motion picture]. USA: Warner Brothers Pictures.

Horwitz, H. (Producer). N/A. (1966). *Batman* [Television series]. USA: Greenway Productions.

Internet Movie Database. (1997) *Batman & Robin* [Motion Picture]. Retrieved from http://www.imdb.com/title/tt0118688/

Ip, J. (2012). The dark knight's war on terrorism [Abstract]. *Ohio State Journal of Criminal Law, 9*(1), 209-229. Retrieved from http://moritzlaw.osu.edu/students/groups/osjcl/files/2012/05/Ip.pdf

Jones, J. (2008, August). *Converting to terrorism: What the psychology of religion tells us about religiously motivated terrorism* [Abstract]. Annual Meeting of the American Psychological Association, 1-23. Retrieved from http://www.bloodthatcriesout.com/sitebuildercontent/sitebuilderfiles/terrorismconversionpaper2.pdf

Jung, B. (2010). *Narrating violence in post-9/11 action cinema: Terrorist narratives, cinematic narration, and referentiality.* doi:10.1007/978-3-531-92602-5

Kagan, K., Kagan, F. W. (2011, May 3). An unusually hard target. *The New York Times.* Retrieved from http://www.nytimes.com

Katzman, S. (Producer), Bennet, S. (Director). (1949). *Batman and Robin* [Film Serial]. USA: Columbia Pictures.

Klavan, A. (2008, July 25). What Bush and Batman have in common. *The Wall Street Journal, Retrieved from* http://online.wsj.com

Kolenic, A. (2009). Madness in the making: Creating and denying narrative from Virginia Tech to Gotham City. *Journal of Popular Culture, 42*(6), 1023-1039. doi: 10.1111/j.1540-5931.2009.00720.x

Marsh, J. (1999). Batman and Batwoman go to school: Popular culture in the literacy curriculum. *International Journal of Early Years Education, 7*(2), 117-131. doi:10.1080/0966976990070201

Mayerfeld, J. (2008, April). In defense of the absolute prohibition of torture. *Public Affairs Quarterly, 22*(2), 109-128. Retrieved from http://faculty.washington.edu/jasonm/4--Mayerfeld.indd.pdf

Metz, C. (2004). Film language: Problems of denotation in fiction film. *Film Theory and Criticism,* 72-86. New York, NY: Oxford University Press.

Morrison, G. (2011). *Supergods: What masked vigilantes, miraculous mutants, and a sun god from Smallville can teach us about being human.* New York, NY: Spiegel & Grau.

Nelson, J. S. (2008). Realism as a political style: Noir insights. *POROI: Assorted Topics with a Poroi Symposium on Visual Citizens, 5*(2), 1-46. Retrieved from http://ir.uiowa.edu/cgi/viewcontent.cgi?article=1014&context=poroi

Palmer, B.D. (1997). Night in the capitalist, cold war city: Noir and the cultural politics of darkness. *Left History, 5*(2), 57-76. Retrieved from https://pi.library.yorku.ca/ojs/index.php/lh/article/view/5337

Paul, J., & Park, S. (2009). With the best of intentions: The color coded homeland security advisory system and the law of unintended consequences. *Research and Practice in Social Sciences, 4*(2), 1-13. Retrieved from http://www.researchgate.net/publication/229001775_With_the_best_of_intentions_The_color_coded_homeland_security_advisory_system_and_the_law_of_unintended_consequences

Reboul, A. (2006). Intercultural pragmatics and the clash of civilizations: Western and Muslim interactions before and since 9/11 [Abstract]. *Intercultural Pragmatics 3-4,* 465-485. Retrieved from http://l2c2.isc.cnrs.fr/publications/files/intercultural-prag.pdf

Rodriguez, M. (2010). Physiognomy & freakery: The Joker on film. *Annenberg School, Conference Papers--International Communication Association,* 1-26. Retrieved, from http://citation.allacademic.com/meta/p_mla_apa_research_citation/4/0/3/6/3/p403632_index.html

Rudolph, C., F. (Producer), Hillyer, L. (Director). (1943). *Batman* [Film Serial]. USA: Columbia Pictures.

Russell, D.J. (1998). Monster roundup: Reintegrating the horror genre. *Refiguring American Film Genres,* 233-254. Berkeley, CA: University of California Press.

Schatz, T. (1981). *Hollywood Genres.* New York, NY: McGraw-Hill.

Scheppele, K. L. (2004). Law in a time of emergency: States of exception and the temptations of 9/11. *University of Pennsylvania Journal of Constitutional Law, 6,* 1001-1083. Retrieved from http://papers.ssrn.com/sol3/papers.cfm?abstract_id=611884

Schlesinger, A. (2010). Holy economic history of the American comic book industry, Batman! (Honors thesis). Retrieved from http://wesscholar.wesleyan.edu/etd_hon_theses/429/

Shane, S., & Savage, C. (2011, May 3). Bin laden raid revives debate on value of torture. *The New York Times.* Retrieved from http://www.nytimes.com

Simone M. A. (2009). Give me liberty and give me surveillance: A case study of the U.S. government's disclosure of surveillance. *Critical Discourse Studies, 6*(1), 1-14. Retrieved from http://www.tandfonline.com/doi/abs/10.1080/17405900802559977#preview

Smith, B. (2009). Spandex cinema: Three approaches to comic book film adaptation (Master's thesis). Retrieved from http://library.uco.edu/UCOthesis/SmithBP2009.pdf

Sobchack, V. (1998). Lounge time: Postwar crisis and the chronotope of film noir. *Refiguring American Films Genres*. Berkeley, CA: University of California Press.

Thomas, E., Franco, L. J., Roven, C., Melniker, B., & Uslan, M. (Producers), Nolan, C. (Director). (2005). *Batman Begins* [Motion picture]. USA: Warner Brothers Pictures.

Thomas, E., Roven, C., Melniker, B., Uslan, M., & Nolan, C. (Producers), Nolan, C. (Director). (2008). *The Dark Knight* [Motion picture]. USA: Warner Brothers Pictures.

Tuman, J. S. (2010). *Communicating terror: The rhetorical dimensions of terrorism (2nd ed.)*. Thousand Oaks, CA: SAGE Publications.

Vernet, M. (1999). The filmic transaction: On the openings of films noirs. *Film Noir Reader 2, 57-71*. New York, NY: Limelight Editions.

Wanzo, R. (2009). The superhero: Meditations on surveillance, salvation, and desire. *Communication and Critical/Cultural Studies. 6*(1). doi: 10.1080/14791420802663694

Zehnder, S., & Calvert, S. (2003). *Developmental differences in younger and older adolescents? Understanding of heroism.* Northwestern University & Georgetown University, Conference Papers--International Communication Association, San Diego, CA, 1-28. Retrieved from http://citation.allacademic.com/meta/p_mla_apa_research_citation/1/1/2/2/3/pages112230/p112230-1.php

Zinnbaurer, B., & Paragarment, K. (1998). Spiritual conversion: A study of religious change among college students. *Journal for the Scientific Study of Religion, 37*(1), *161-180*. Retrieved from http://www.psychology.hku.hk/ftbcstudies/refbase/docs/zinnbauer/1998/66_Zinnbauer+Pargament1998.pdf

www.ingramcontent.com/pod-product-compliance
Lightning Source LLC
Chambersburg PA
CBHW070158230526
45471CB00002B/723